TONY BUZAN®

THE *BUZAN*® STUDY SKILLS HANDBOOK

Other Tony Buzan titles published by BBC Active:

Buzan Bites
Mind Mapping
Speed Reading
Brilliant Memory

The Mind Set
Use Your Head
Use Your Memory
Master Your Memory
The Speed Reading Book
The Mind Map® Book
The Illustrated Mind Map® Book

Embracing Change

TONY BUZAN™

THE *BUZAN*™ STUDY SKILLS HANDBOOK

CONSULTANT EDITOR JAMES HARRISON

BBC ACTIVE

BBC Active, an imprint of Educational Publishers LLP, part of the Pearson Education Group
Edinburgh Gate,
Harlow,
Essex
CM20 2JE,
England

First published in 2007 by BBC Active
Fifth impression 2009

ISBN 978 1 4066 1207 3

Commissioning Editor: Emma Shackleton
Consultant Editor: James Harrison
Project Editor: Jeanette Payne
Text Designer: Annette Peppis
Cover Designer: R&D&Co Design Ltd
Senior Production Controller: Man Fai Lau
Illustrations: Alan Burton
Printed and bound by China CTPSC/05

The Publisher's policy is to use paper manufactured from sustainable forests.

CONTENTS

Introduction

The *Buzan Study Skills Handbook* comprises the unique BOST® (Buzan Organic Study Technique) programme, designed specifically to improve any student's capabilities to prepare for those dreaded higher school, college and university exams, essays, tests, modules and coursework generally.

This handbook will help you overcome your quite rational fears about exams and pressured study, and you will discover in these pages a new and totally positive way to learn, using your fantastic brain and mind power.

It is no mere boast. The BOST programme has been honed from 35 years' experience in the field of study skills, brain power, recall after learning, Radiant Thinking® techniques, concentration, and the multi-dimensional memory tool; the Mind Map®. The structured skills set out here will quite literally enhance your capabilities in leaps and bounds to:

- Prepare with confidence for study, exams and tests.
- Read far more quickly and efficiently than you thought possible.
- Note-take and note-make even more effectively.
- Memorize and recall what you have learnt far more successfully.
- Get into a revision mind-set but still enjoy 'time outs' to relax.
- Increase your revising capacity dramatically using Mind Maps (described as 'the Swiss army knife of the brain').

Incorporating the unique BOST programme, this handbook will provide you with the confidence *and* the means to fulfil your own study potential – whatever your subjects or academic level.

Fear and loathing of exams and revision

If you're sceptical (and why wouldn't you be?), before you even turn a page, ask yourself this:

- Do I fear exams?
- Am I a reluctant learner?
- Am I daunted about the amount of studying I have to do?
- Do I do everything except getting down to revising?
- Do I displace time rather than plan it?
- Do I find it hard to retain, remember and recall information?
- Do I feel I have to study a reference cover to cover in order to grasp it?
- Do I work when I'm too tired or distracted?
- Do I believe the best way to absorb information is to read a text top to bottom, cover to cover?
- Do I learn by rote without really understanding?

My guess is that you have answered yes to at least one (if not all!) of these questions, making this study skills guide the ideal tool for perfecting your studying techniques.

Whatever exam you are studying for in higher education, chances are you are not storing and retrieving information, data, facts and figures and reference as quickly and effectively as you have the potential to do.

This may be because of:

- Lack of motivation.
- Accumulation of bad studying habits.
- No 'game plan' for revising and note-taking specific essays, exams, projects, subjects or papers.
- Apprehension and anxiety about pressures of time and amount of study.
- No 'Operations Manual' for your brain.

Your fears – and they are entirely rational – and feelings of negativity are something you look at, you admit, you accept, you know that everybody else feels them and, by the way, they're totally unnecessary.

The downward spiral of study fear

Imagine this scenario (if it hasn't happened to you already): the teacher slams the book 'bang!' on the table and says this is the book you will be examined on, this is your test book, and if you don't do well on this book and if you don't understand every single concept in these pages then you will fail. So take it home and read it slowly and carefully...

And that's what you do... it weighs a lot physically, and mentally it *is* a lot. Then all sorts of evasive actions or displacement activities kick in: you go to the fridge, you watch TV, you txt msg friends and finally you sit down with the tome. What then happens?

If you read for two hours – a long time – at normal study speeds with habitual breaks in concentration, you're probably reading a page in maybe five minutes and taking notes, very often for ten minutes, so after two hours in which you are already forgetting what you read, you cover a tiny fraction of the book. And you can physically *see* how little you've covered: it's been hard, laborious, you've got eye-ache, ear-ache, head-ache, neck-ache, back-ache, bum-ache, all the aches, and you've got that much to go and you know you're going to forget most of it. As you go through your horrible linear notes week-in, week-out, month-in, month-out, forgetting as you go along like scattering seeds that die as you sew, and the examinations are looming, you know you're doomed – and your are.

You get demoralized and say, 'Sod this for a lark,' and you go and have a beer. And then it's a slippery slide to crib notes, asking friends, scouring the web, trying to make the professor or teacher give something away. All this is entirely rationally based, because you are right: this type of study is fundamentally a waste of time. You must learn how to do it properly.

Now you *can*, if you work through and practise with the *Buzan Study Skills Handbook*. Your negative spiral will become a positive, motivating experience.

How to do it: how to get the most from this study guide

Every part of this book should be the first page – when structuring this book it became apparent that any chapter could be 'Chapter 1' because everything is vitally important. So I suggest you first skim through the various chapters of this book to 'get a feel' for the contents and approach, and then take a closer look at each chapter. Each one deals with a different aspect of your brain's functioning and gives you different ways to unlock and harness it as an exponentially more effective study tool.

Chapter 1: Your brain: it's better than you think, *really*

shows you what an amazing instrument for study your brain is and **can be** for you. Case studies of students who have used the BOST programme are highlighted to show its application and versatility in different study scenarios. It explains how you should never underestimate your own potential, and how you can unlock the incredible capacity of your brain.

Chapter 2: Obstacles to effective study examines the mental, emotional and physical 'blocks' and barriers to effective study so that you can relate to them and not feel intimidated by the weight of expectation as exams loom. The core skills of the BOST programme are then set out in the subsequent chapters.

Chapter 3: BOST® gives you the simple-to-follow eight-point BOST strategy for study **Preparation and Application**. Preparation includes the key skills of browsing, time management, refreshing memory and defining questions and goals, while Application is divided into the Overview, Preview, Inview and Review skills.

Chapter 4: Speed reading. Do you read so slowly that you're falling asleep in the university library? You obviously need to speed up your reading and comprehension of what you are studying and revising. This chapter is much more than just grasping a technique: it also shows you how to concentrate, how to skim and scan data and, critically, how your studying environment and posture influence your propensity and desire to learn. This chapter will help you save time and study more efficiently. As you bring speed reading skills to the core of your revision studies alongside Mind Mapping (see Chapters 6 and 7) and harnessing your memory (Chapter 5) your confidence will also increase.

In **Chapter 5: Supercharge your memory** I am going to teach the main techniques you need to use to remember, and these techniques will support what you go on to learn about Mind Mapping in Chapters 6 and 7. I explain how you can improve memory both **during** and **after learning**. In addition, two Key Memory Systems to assist your studies are introduced for the perfect memorization of listed items.

Chapter 6: Mind Maps® lays out this unique memory, recall and revision method that echoes your mind's internal 'maps'. The Mind Map is a multi-dimensional memory jogger and a fantastic revision tool. Understanding the way you think will help you to use words and imagery in Mind Map formats for recording, revising, recalling, remembering, organizing, creative thinking and problem solving in your studies and when revising for exams. You must also be able to store, recall and retrieve information and data effectively.

Chapter 7: Revolutionize your study with Mind Maps® and BOST® is your final step along the pathway to success. Here you will learn how to apply your finely tuned Mind Mapping techniques to all aspects of your study. You will learn how to Mind Map your textbooks, DVDs and lecture notes, and you will discover the benefits of Mind Mapping in group study.

Remember to revisit the core skills that you feel need refreshing and **not** to treat the *Buzan Study Skills Handbook* in a totally linear cover-to-cover fashion. I'll stress it again: every part of this book should be the first page. It is also essential that you practise if you wish to be able to use effectively the methods and information laid out in the *Buzan Study Skills Handbook*. At various stages in the book are exercises and suggestions for further activity. In addition you should work out your own practice and study schedule, keeping to it as firmly as possible.

Having gathered the core components of the BOST programme, you can then incorporate all these previous areas of knowledge into a comprehensive study mind set:

⊙ To study hyper-efficiently.

⊙ To organize effectively.

⊙ To read every study book at minimally twice your previous speed.

⊙ To remember what you have learned twice as well.

⊙ To Mind Map your books and notes in such a way that you will be able to remember your subjects four to ten times better.

So get ready to fulfil your real potential for effective and successful study with the aid of the BOST programme – incorporating speed reading, Mind Mapping and memory recall – the ultimate combination of study skills tapping in to **your** greatest asset, that is, your brain.

Let me know of your success!

1 YOUR BRAIN: IT'S BETTER THAN YOU THINK, *REALLY*

Your brain is an extraordinary, super-powered processor capable of boundless and interconnected thoughts: if only you know how to harness it, studying will cease to be a fraught and stressful exercise, and will be fast, easy and fruitful.

Your amazing brain began to evolve over 500 million years ago, but it's only in the last 500 years that we've discovered that it is located in your head, and not your stomach or heart (as Aristotle and a lot other famous scientists believed). Even more amazing is the fact that 95 per cent of what we know about your brain and how it works was discovered within the last ten years. We have so much more to learn.

Your brain has five major functions:

1   **Receiving** – Your brain receives information via your senses.

2   **Storing** – Your brain retains and stores the information and is able to access it on demand. (Although it may not always feel that way to you!)

3   **Analyzing** – Your brain recognizes patterns and likes to organize information in ways that make sense: by examining information and questioning meaning.

4   **Controlling** – Your brain controls the way you manage information in different ways, depending upon your state of health, your personal attitude and your environment.

5   **Outputting** – Your brain outputs received information through thoughts, speech, drawing, movement, and all other forms of creativity.

The techniques laid out in the *Buzan Study Skills Handbook* will help you utilize these brain skills by helping your brain to learn, analyze, store and retrieve information effectively and on demand.

The man with two brains

How your brain manages these superfast processes is even more astounding. The breakthrough discovery is knowing now that we have two upper brains rather than one, and that they operate in different degrees in the different mental areas. The two sides of your brain, or your two cortices as they are called, are linked by a fantastically complex network of nerve fibres known as the *Corpus Callosum*, and deal dominantly with different types of mental activity.

right 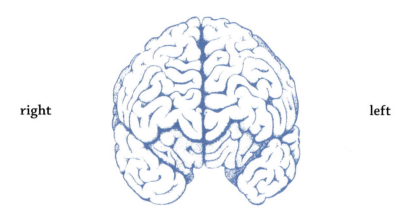 **left**

In most people the **left cortex** deals with:

⊙ logic, words, lists, lines, numbers and analysis – the so-called 'academic' activities. While the left cortex is engaged in these activities, the right cortex is more in the 'alpha wave' or resting state, ready to assist.

The **right cortex** deals with:

⊙ rhythm, imagination, colour, daydreaming, spatial awareness, Gestalt (that is, the whole organized picture or, as you might put it, 'the whole being greater than the sum of its parts') and dimension.

Subsequent research has shown that when people were encouraged to develop a mental area they had previously considered weak, this development, rather than detracting from other areas, seemed to produce a synergetic effect in which all areas of mental performance improved. Moreover, each hemisphere contains many more of the other side's abilities than had been thought previously, and each hemisphere also is capable of a much wider and much more subtle range of mental activities.

Einstein, for instance, failed French at school and numbered among his activities violin playing, art, sailing, and 'imagination games'. And Einstein gave credit for many of his more significant scientific insights to those imagination games. While daydreaming on a hill one summer day, he imagined riding sunbeams to the far extremities of the Universe, and upon finding himself returned, 'illogically', to the surface of the sun, he realized that the Universe must indeed be curved, and that his previous 'logical' training was incomplete. The numbers, equations and words he wrapped around this new image gave us the Theory of Relativity – a **left and right cortex synthesis**.

Similarly the great artists turned out to be 'whole-brained'. Rather than note books filled with stories of drunken parties, and paint slapped on haphazardly to produce masterpieces, entries similar to the following were found:

> **Up at 6 a.m. Spent seventeenth day on painting number six of the latest series. Mixed four parts orange with two parts yellow to produce a colour combination which I placed in upper left-hand corner of canvas, to act in**

visual opposition to spiral structures in lower right-hand corner, producing desired balance in eye of perceiver.

Telling examples of just how much left-cortex activity goes into what we normally consider right-cortex pursuits.

The other Da Vinci Code

One man in the last thousand years stands out as a supreme example of what a human being can do if both cortical sides of the brain are developed simultaneously: Leonardo da Vinci. In his time he was arguably the most accomplished man in each of the following disciplines: art, sculpture, physiology, general science, architecture, mechanics, anatomy, physics, invention, meteorology, geology, engineering and aviation. He could also play, compose and sing spontaneous ballads when thrown any stringed instrument in the courts of Europe. Rather than separating these different areas of his latent ability, da Vinci combined them. His scientific note books are filled with three-dimensional drawings and images; and, equally interesting, the final plans for his great painting masterpieces often look like architectural plans: straight lines, angles, curves and numbers incorporating mathematics, logic and precise measurements.

Fulfilling your mental potential

It seems, then, that when we describe ourselves as talented in certain areas and not talented in others, what we are really describing are those areas of our potential that we have successfully developed, and those areas of our potential that still lie dormant, which in reality could – with the right nurturing – flourish.

The two sides of your brain do not operate separately from one another – they need to work together to be at their most effective. The more you can stimulate both sides of your brain at the same time, the more effectively they will work together to help you to:

- Think better.
- Remember more.
- Recall instantly.

Stimulation for study is going to come in the guise of BOST, the Buzan Organic Study Technique programme. Using these unique and personally refined study skills – incorporating Mind Maps, Radiant Thinking, Speed Reading, Recall after Learning and other core Buzan Study Skills– your ability to master revision, learning, comprehension, exam study and preparation will be transformed. Consider, to give you confidence, these two true student cases studies:

Case study – Eva

'Nobody should ever be told he or she is stupid or that they can't do something. We all have potential and it is vital that every person studying is given the best opportunity to achieve that potential. But we need ways that work for us. Tony Buzan's techniques are incredibly powerful and yet simple to learn and I strongly advocate young people being given an introduction to them at school and college, so they can maximize their enjoyment of learning.'

Eva, a researcher who transformed her study techniques through Mind Mapping.

Eva had a tough schooling: her school had relegated her to the 'dumb pile' and pretty explicitly told her parents she didn't have 'a hope in hell' of passing her exams. Eva, bluntly, was regarded as stupid, but in fact she was dyslexic (a condition much better known about now). Moreover, she loved learning, and after an assessment by an educational psychologist when she was 13 she knew she had an above average IQ. *'So I knew that I had to learn in a different way,' says Eva. 'My reaction to being told I was stupid and wouldn't get my 'A' Levels was to work harder to prove them wrong... I can be very stubborn.'*

Eva was 16 when she discovered Mind Maps in the first year of her 'A' Levels. She was lucky to find a truly inspirational tutor and her parents were incredibly supportive and had real belief in her. It was her mum who found the tutor who viewed Eva as 'potential' rather than 'work', and discovered who she was and how she worked best. Eva's tutor taught her Mind Mapping and opened up a new world of learning possibilities.

'The visual appeal was huge and my organizational demon liked having everything on one page,' recalls Eva.

The Mind Maps were invaluable in all her studies from 'A' levels through to her professional qualifications in marketing.

'In my studies I consistently achieved high results including many distinctions and merits. In one exam I got the highest mark in the country (CAM Advertising paper).'

As Eva concludes: *'School went a long way to dampen my love of learning to the point at which the idea of three more years at University was a horror to me – which is very sad as I know I would have loved it. Tony Buzan's Mind Maps and learning techniques reintroduced that love of learning which I cherish to this day.'*

Case study – Edmund

At the age of 11 years and still at his prep school, Edmund was clear in his dream. He wanted to go to Winchester College, one of the leading academic public schools in the UK. But in order to reach this goal, he had to work hard to achieve the high grades that Winchester demands. Nine months before he sat his Common Entrance exams his grades were not high enough and the target seemed far off. His mother, knowing the work of Tony Buzan and all his learning-how-to-learn techniques, set about teaching Edmund how to do Mind Maps and how to apply them to his school work. This was a turning point for him and very quickly, instead of feeling overwhelmed by the eight subjects that he knew he had to pass, Edmund felt in control and was able to plan his revision and study periods. First, he created a Mind Map on the eight subjects, which gave him the 'overview' he needed to recognize which subject needed more work. Then he created a Mind Map for each subject, giving a branch to the main topic headings in that subject. Thus, on just a single piece of paper, he had the whole syllabus for that one subject and could concentrate on the topics that he felt needed more revision or work. When the exams eventually came, instead of feeling a sense of panic, he was able to organize his thoughts and answers through the use of rough Mind Maps. The result was a resounding success. Edmund passed all of his exams with ease and went to the school of his dreams.

2   OBSTACLES TO EFFECTIVE STUDY

You have this fantastic mind, this awesome brain power, so why do you feel fear, stress and anxiety when it comes to studying?

Most people will have experienced difficulties in studying or revising for examinations. This chapter outlines these common difficulties so that you can accept and overcome your quite rational fears of the exam, test, assessment, essay, thesis and coursework. The key barriers to successful study are:

- **The reluctant learner.**
- **The mental blocks to effective study.**
- **Outdated study techniques.**

The reluctant learner

The Six-o'clock-in-the-Evening-Enthusiastic-Determined-and-Well-Intentioned-Studier-Until-Midnight is a person with whom you are probably already familiar. At 6 p.m. the student approaches his (or her) desk, and carefully organizes everything in preparation for the study period to follow. Having everything in place, he next carefully adjusts each item again, giving him time to complete the first excuse; he recalls that in the morning he did not have quite enough time to read all articles of interest in the newspaper. He also realizes that if he is going to study it is best to have such small things completely out of the way before settling down to the task at hand.

He therefore leaves his desk, browses through the newspaper and notices as he browses that there are more articles of interest than he had originally thought. He also notices, as he leafs through the pages, the entertainment section. At this point it seems like a good idea to plan for the evening's first break – perhaps an interesting programme between 8 and 8.30 p.m.

He finds the programme, and it inevitably starts at about 7 p.m. At this point, he thinks, 'Well, I've had a difficult day and it's not too long before the programme starts, and I need a rest anyway and the relaxation will really help me to get down to studying...' He returns to his desk at 7.45 p.m, because the beginning of the next programme was also a bit more interesting than he thought it would be.

At this stage, he still hovers over his desk, tapping his book reassuringly as he remembers that phone call and text messaging to his two fellow students which, like the articles of interest in the newspaper, are best cleared out of the way before the serious studying begins.

The phone call and texts coming back and forth, of course, are much more interesting and longer than originally planned, but eventually the intrepid studier finds himself back at his desk at about 8.30 p.m.

At this point in the proceedings he actually sits down at the desk, opens the book with a display of physical determination and starts to read (usually at page one) as he experiences the first pangs of hunger and thirst. This is disastrous because he realizes that the longer he waits to satisfy the pangs, the worse they will get, and the more interrupted his study concentration will be.

The obvious and only solution is a light snack, but as more and more tasty items are linked to the central core of hunger, the snack becomes a feast.

Having removed this final obstacle, he returns to his desk with the certain knowledge that this time there is nothing that could possibly interfere with the dedication. The first couple of sentences on page one are looked at again... as the studier realizes that his stomach is feeling decidedly heavy and a general drowsiness seems to have set in. Far better at this juncture to watch that other interesting half-hour programme at 10 p.m., after which the digestion will be mostly completed and the rest will enable him really to get down to the task at hand.

At midnight we find him asleep in front of the TV.

Even at this point, when he has been woken up by whoever comes into the room, he will think that things have not gone too badly, for after all he had a good rest, a good meal, watched some interesting and relaxing programmes, fulfilled his social commitments to his friends, digested the day's information, and got everything completely out of the way so that *tomorrow*, at 6 p.m...

Fear of (coming to grips with) study is rational.

At the present time information is being given more importance and emphasis than the individual. As a result, the reluctant learner is being mentally swamped and almost literally 'weighed down' by it all. Both the information and publication explosions are still continuing at staggering rates, while the ability of the individual to handle and study it all remains neglected. If he is ever to cope with the situation he must learn not more 'hard facts', but new ways of handling and studying the information – new ways of using his natural abilities to learn, think, recall, create and find solutions to problems.

The mental blocks to effective study

The preceding episode is probably familiar and amusing, but the implications of it are significant and serious.

On one level the story is encouraging because, by the very fact that it is a problem experienced by everybody, it confirms what has long been suspected: that everyone is creative and inventive, and that the feelings that many have about being uncreative are not necessary. The creativity demonstrated in the example of the reluctant student is not applied very usefully. But the diversity and originality with which we all make up reasons for *not* doing things suggests that each person has a wealth of talent which could be applied in more positive directions!

On another level the story is discouraging because it shows up the widespread and underlying fear that most of us experience when confronted with a study text.

This reluctance and fear arises from the examination-based education system in which the student is presented with textbooks on the subjects he is 'taking'. He knows that textbooks are 'harder' than storybooks and novels; he also knows that they represent a lot of work; and he further knows that he will be tested on his knowledge of the information from the books.

So:

1   The fact that the type of book is 'hard' is discouraging in itself.

2   The fact that the book represents work is also discouraging, because the student instinctively knows that he is unable to read, note, and remember properly.

3   The fact that he is going to be tested is often the most serious of the three difficulties. It is well known that this threat can completely disrupt your brain's ability to work in certain situations. The number of cases are legion of people who literally cannot write anything in an exam situation despite the fact that they know their subject thoroughly – as are the number of cases of people who, even though they are able to write some form of answer, have gigantic mental blocks where whole areas of knowledge are completely forgotten during an exam period. In even more extreme cases many people have been known to spend a whole two-hour period writing frantically, assuming that they were answering the question, when in fact they are repeating over and over again either their own name or one word.

Faced with this kind of threat, which for many is truly terrifying, the student has one of two choices: he can either study and face one set of consequences, or not study and face a different set of consequences. If he studies and does badly, then he has proven himself 'incapable', 'unintelligent', 'stupid', a 'dunce', or whatever the negative expression is at the time.

Of course this is not really the case, but he has no way of knowing that it is the system which is not testing him properly, and not his own ineptitude causing the 'failure'.

If he does not study, the situation is quite different. Confronted with having failed a test or exam, he can immediately say that obviously he failed it because he 'didn't study and wasn't interested in that kind of stuff anyway'.

By doing this, the reluctant student solves the problem in a number of ways:

⊙ He avoids both the test and the threat to his self-esteem that studying would involve.

⊙ He has a perfect excuse for failing.

⊙ He gets respect from fellow students because he is daring to attack a situation which is frightening to them as well. It is interesting to note that such a student will often find himself in the position of a leader.

It is also interesting to note that even those who do make the decision to study will still reserve a little part of themselves for behaving like the non-studier. The person who gets scores as high as 80 or 90 per cent will also be found using exactly the same excuses for not getting 100 per cent as the non-studier uses for failing.

Outdated study techniques

The situations described are unsatisfactory for everyone concerned. One further and major reason for poor study results lies in the way we have approached both study techniques and the information we wanted people to study.

We have surrounded the person with a confusing mass of different subjects or 'disciplines', demanding that he learn,

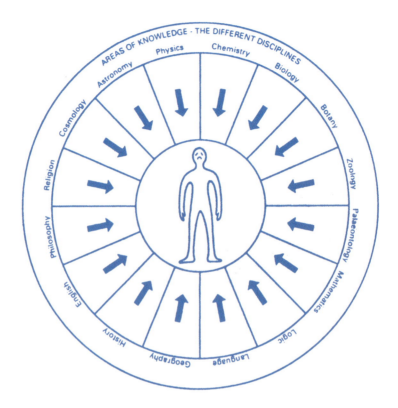

In traditional education, information is given or 'taught' about the different areas of knowledge that surround the individual. The direction and flow is from the subject to the individual – he is simply given the information, and is expected to absorb, learn and remember as much as he possibly can.

remember and understand a frightening array of subjects under headings such as Mathematics, Physics, Chemistry, Biology, Zoology, Botany, Anatomy, Physiology, Sociology, Psychology, Anthropology, Philosophy, History, Geography, English, Media Studies, Music, Technology and Palaeontology. In each of these subject areas the individual has been and is still presented with series of dates, theories, facts, names, and general ideas.

What this really means is that we have been taking a totally lopsided approach to study and to the way in which a person deals with and relates to the information and knowledge that surrounds him.

As can be seen from the illustration, we are concentrating far too much on information about the 'separate' areas of knowledge. We are also laying too much stress on asking the individual to feed back facts in pre-digested order or in pre-set forms such as standard examination papers or formal essays.

This approach has also been reflected in the standard study techniques recommended in sixth form colleges, universities, institutes of further education and the text and study books that go with it. These techniques have been 'grid' approaches in which it is recommended that a series of steps always be worked through on any book being studied. One common suggestion is that any reasonably difficult study book should always be read through three times in order to ensure a complete understanding. This is obviously a very simple example, but even the many more developed approaches tend to be comparatively rigid and inflexible – simply standard systems to be repeated on each studying occasion.

It is obvious that methods such as these cannot be applied with success to every study book. There is an enormous difference between studying a text on Literary Criticism and studying a text on Higher Mathematics. In order to study properly, a technique is required which does not force the same approach to such different materials.

First, it is necessary to start working from the individual outwards. Rather than bombarding him with books, formulas and examinations we must begin to concentrate on teaching each person how he or she can study most efficiently. We must teach

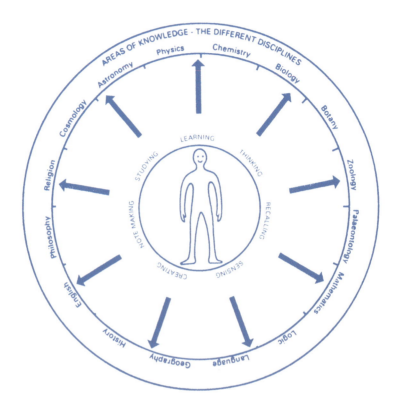

In the new forms of education, the previous emphases must be reversed. Instead of teaching the individual facts about other things, we must first teach him facts about himself – facts about how he can learn, think, recall, create, solve problems, and so on.

ourselves how our eyes work when we read, how we remember, how we think, how we can learn more effectively, how we can organize noting, how we can solve problems and in general how we can best use our abilities, whatever the subject matter (see illustration on above).

Most of the problems outlined here will be eliminated when we finally do change the emphasis away from the subject toward the student and how he can select and understand any information he wants to. Students will be equipped to study and remember whatever area of knowledge is interesting or necessary. Things will not have to be 'crammed in'. Each student will be able to range subjects at his own pace, going for help and personal supervision only when he realizes it is necessary.

Yet another advantage of this approach is that it will make both teaching and learning much easier, more enjoyable and more productive. By concentrating on individuals and their abilities, we will finally and sensibly have placed the learning situation in its proper perspective.

Onword

One is tempted to note here that the modern student has access to instruction manuals and 'How To Do It' books and websites on virtually anything he wishes to study or research. But when it comes to the most complicated, complex, and important organism of all, ourselves, there has been practically no help. We need our own 'operations manual' on how to operate our own 'Super Bio Computer'. The *Buzan Study Skills Handbook* is that operations manual.

3 BOST®

The Buzan Organic Study Technique (BOST®), laid out in this chapter, will show you how to develop strong study habits and overcome those study fears, stresses and anxieties. In the following four chapters, we are going to reinforce and multiply the power of the technique by introducing you to ways of increasing your speed while using it. This will improve your memory of what you read, as you read it and after you've read it. The master note-taking technique, the Mind Map® will allow you to have everything you have speed read and everything you have learned and remembered in order, perfectly structured and under control. In the final chapter, we will revisit BOST and supplement it and empower it with each of these major elements.

BOST is divided into two main strategies: **Preparation** and **Application**.

It is important to note at the outset that although the main steps are presented in a certain order, this order is by no means essential and can be changed, subtracted from and added to as the study texts warrant. You will also need to read and revisit the chapters on Speed Reading, Memory and Mind Maps to utilize the BOST programme for maximum effect.

BOST®: Preparation

This first section contains:
- **The browse.**
- **Time and amount.**
- **Five minute Mind Map jotter.**
- **Asking questions and defining goals.**

The browse

Before doing anything else, it is essential to 'browse' or look through the entire textbook, journal, lecture notes or periodical you are about to study. The browse should be done in the way you would look through a book you were considering buying in a book shop, or considering taking out from the library. In other words, casually but rather rapidly flipping through the pages, getting the general 'feel' of the book, observing the organization and structure, the level of difficulty, the proportion of diagrams and illustrations to text, and the location of any Results, Summaries and Conclusions.

Time and amount

These two aspects can be dealt with simultaneously because the theory behind them both is similar.

The first thing to do when sitting down to study a textbook is to decide on the periods of time to be devoted to it. Having done this, decide what amount to cover in each time period.

The reason for insisting on these two initial steps is not arbitrary, and is supported by the findings of the Gestalt psychologists. (Before reading on, complete the activity on page 40.)

The Gestalt psychologists discovered that the human brain has a very strong tendency to complete things – thus most readers will find that they labelled the shapes on page 40 as straight line, cylinder, square, ellipse or oval, zigzag line, circle, triangle, wavy or curved line, rectangle. In fact the 'circle' is not a circle but a 'broken circle'. Many actually see this broken circle as a completed circle. Others see it as a broken circle but assume that the artist intended to complete it.

1

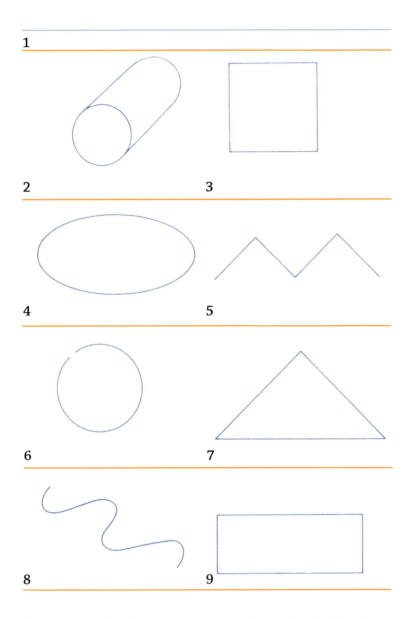

2

3

4

5

6

7

8

9

Shape recognition. Enter the name of the shape of each of the items above next to the appropriate number.

In study, making a decision about Time and Amount gives us a secure anchor, as well as an end point, or goal. This has the advantage of enabling the proper linkages to be made rather than encouraging a wandering off in more disconnected ways.

An excellent comparison is that of listening to a good lecturer. She, attempting to expound a lot of difficult material, will usually explain her starting and ending points and will often indicate the amount of time to be spent on each area of the presentation. The audience will automatically find the lecture easier to follow because they have guidelines within which to work.

It is advisable to define physically the amount to be read by placing reasonably large paper markers at the beginning and end of the section chosen. This enables you to refer back and forward to the information in the chosen amount.

A further advantage of making these decisions at the outset is that the underlying fear of the unknown is avoided. If a large study book is plunged into with no planning, the number of pages you eventually have to complete will continuously oppress you. Each time you sit down you will be aware that you still have 'a few hundred pages to go' and will be studying with this as a constant and real background threat. If, on the other hand, you have selected a reasonable number of pages for the time you are going to study, you will be reading with the knowledge that the task you have set yourself is easy and can certainly be completed. The difference in attitude and performance will be marked.

The five minute Mind Map® jotter

Having decided on the amounts to be covered, next jot down as fast as you can everything you know on the subject. No more than five minutes should be devoted to the exercise.

The purpose of this exercise is:

- ⊙ To improve concentration.
- ⊙ To eliminate wandering.
- ⊙ To establish a good mental 'set'.

This last term refers to getting your mind filled with important rather than unimportant information. If you have spent five minutes searching your memory for pertinent information, you will be far more attuned to the text material and far less likely to continue thinking about the strawberries and cream you are going to eat afterwards.

From the time limit of five minutes on this exercise it is obvious that your entire knowledge is not required – the five-minute exercise is intended purely to activate your storage system and to set your mind off in the right direction.

One question which will arise is 'what about the difference in my Mind Map if I know almost nothing on the subject or if I know an enormous amount?'

If knowledge in the area is great, the five minutes should be spent recalling the major divisions, theories and names connected with the subject. As your mind can flash through information much faster than your hand can write it, all the minor associations will still be 'seen' mentally and the proper mental set and direction will be established.

If the knowledge of the subject is almost nothing, the five minutes should be spent recalling those few items which are known, as well as any other information which seems in any way at all to be connected. This will enable you to get as close as you possibly can to the new subject, and will prevent you from feeling totally lost as so many do in this situation.

So, you gain by gathering together your immediate and current state of knowledge on areas of interest. In this way you will be able to keep much more up to date with yourself and will actually know what you know, rather than being in a continually embarrassing position of not knowing what you know – the 'I've got it on the tip of my tongue' syndrome.

Asking questions and defining goals

Having established your current state of knowledge on the subject, decide what you want from the book. This involves defining the questions you want answered during the reading, and these questions should refer directly to what you wish to achieve. Many prefer to use a different coloured pen for this section, and add their questions to their jotting of current knowledge. A Mind Map is the best way to do this (see Chapter 6).

This exercise, again like that for noting knowledge, is based on the principle of establishing proper mental sets. It shouldn't take much more than five minutes at the outset, as questions can be redefined and added to as the reading progresses.

Why knowledge and aims are important

A standard experiment to confirm this approach takes two groups of people who are generally equal in terms of age, education and aptitude. Each group is given the same study text and is given enough time to complete the whole book.

Group A is told that they are going to be given a completely comprehensive test on everything in the book and that they must study accordingly.

Group B is told that they will be tested on two or three major themes which run through the book, and that they also must study accordingly.

Both groups are in fact tested on the entire text, a situation that one would immediately think unfair to the group that had been told they would be tested only on the main themes.

One might also think that in this situation the second group would do better on questions about the themes they had been given, the first group better on other questions and that both groups might have a similar final score. To the surprise of many, the second group not only does better on questions about the themes, but *they achieve higher total scores which include better marks on all parts of the test.*

The reason for this is that the main themes act like great grappling hooks through the information, attaching everything else to them. In other words the main questions and goals act as associative and linking centres to which all other information becomes easily attached.

The group instructed to get everything had no centres at all to which they could connect new information, and because of this they groped, with no foundations, through the information. It is much like a situation where a person is given so much choice that he ends up making no decision; the paradox where attempting to get everything gains nothing. Asking questions and establishing goals can be seen, like the section preceding it, to become more and more important as the theory behind becomes better understood. It should be emphasized that the more accurately these questions and goals are established, the better you will perform in the Application section of BOST below.

How to Mind Map this application stage is explained in Chapter 6

BOST®: Application

This second section deals with Application and contains:

- ⊙ **Overview.**
- ⊙ **Preview.**
- ⊙ **Inview.**
- ⊙ **Review.**

Overview

One of the interesting facts about people using study books is that most, when given a new text, start reading on page one. It is not advisable to start reading a new study text on the first page. Here's why.

Imagine that you are a fanatical jigsaw-puzzle-doer. A friend arrives on your doorstep with a gigantic box wrapped in paper and tied with string, and tells you that it's a present: 'the most beautiful and complex jigsaw puzzle yet devised by man!' You thank her, and as you watch her walk away down the front path, you decide that from that moment on you are going to devote yourself entirely to the completion of the puzzle.

Before continuing, note in precise detail the steps you would take from that point on in order to complete the task. Now check your own answers with the following list compiled from my students:

1   Go back inside the house.
2   Take the string off the box.
3   Take off the paper.
4   Dispose of string and paper.
5   Look at the picture on the outside of the box.
6   Read the instructions, concentrating on the number of pieces and overall dimensions of the puzzle.

7 Estimate and organize the amount of time necessary for completion.

8 Plan breaks and meals!

9 Find a surface of appropriate dimensions for the puzzle.

10 Open the box.

11 Empty the contents of the box onto the surface or a separate tray.

12 If pessimistic, check the number of pieces!

13 Turn all the pieces right side up.

14 Find the edge and corner pieces.

15 Sort out colour areas.

16 Fit 'obvious' bits and pieces together.

17 Continue to fill in.

18 Leave 'difficult' pieces until the end (because as the overall picture becomes more clear, and the number of pieces used increases, so does the probability increase that the difficult pieces will fit in more easily when there is greater context into which they can fit).

19 Continue the process until completion.

20 Celebrate!

This jigsaw analogy can be applied directly to study: studying on page one would be like finding the bottom left-hand corner, and insisting to yourself that the entire picture be built up step by step from that corner only!

What is essential in a reasonable approach to study texts, especially difficult ones, is to get a good idea of what's in them before plodding on into a learning catastrophe. The Overview in BOST is designed to perform this task, and may be likened to looking at the picture, reading the instructions, and finding the edge and corner pieces of the puzzle. What this means in the study context is that you should scour the book for all material not included in the regular body of the print, using a visual guide such as a pencil as you do so. Areas of the book to be covered in your overview include:

Results   Tables   Subheadings   Summaries Table of contents   Dates   Conclusions Marginal notes   Italics   Indents Illustrations   Graphs   Glossaries Capitalized words   Footnotes   Back cover Photographs   Statistics

The function of this is to provide you with a good knowledge of the graphic sections of the book, not skimming the whole thing, but selecting specific areas for relatively comprehensive coverage. (Speed reading is a great aid here – see Chapter 4.)

amount of material to be studied

sections to be covered by preview after overview

Sections of a study text to be covered by Overview.

It is extremely important to note again that throughout the overview a pen, pencil, or other form of visual guide, should always be used.

The reason for this can best be explained by reference to a graph. If the eye is unaided, it will simply fixate briefly on general areas of the graph, then move off, leaving only a vague visual memory and an interference to that memory because the eye movement will not have 'registered' the same pattern as the graph.

Example pattern of graph to be studied.

If a visual aid is used, your eye will more closely approximate the flow of the graph and your memory will be strengthened by each of the following inputs:

1   The visual memory itself.

2   The remembered eye movement approximating the graph shape.

3   The memory of the movement of the arm or hand in tracing the graph (Kinaesthetic memory).

4   The visual memory of the rhythm and movement of the tracer.

Standard pattern of unguided eye movement on graph causing conflicting memory of shape of graph.

The overall recall resulting from this practice is far superior to that of a person who reads without any visual guide. It is interesting to note that accountants often use their pens to guide their eyes across and down columns and rows of figures. They do this naturally because any very rigid linear eye movement is difficult to maintain with the unaided eye.

Preview

To preview something means just that: to pre-view, or to *see before*. If you allow your brain to see the whole text before speed reading it (by skimming, in association with one of the guided reading techniques) you will be able to navigate your way through it more effectively when you read it the second time.

The purpose of previewing material before reading it is the same as the purpose of planning a route before driving from A to B. You need to know the terrain and decide whether to take the long scenic route or if a shortcut will suffice.

Previewing should be applied to everything you are studying including communications like exam details and emails. If done effectively it will save you an immense amount of time, and speed up your levels of reading and comprehension.

How to Preview effectively

Be aware of what you already know before you begin reading a book or a document and have an idea of what you want to achieve by reading it. Skim read the text first to discover the core elements. If the text is describing something you know already, make a note of the fact for future reference.

Take effective notes on everything you read so that you can refer back to them in future and use your previously acquired knowledge to assess the relevance of what you are reading.

During the preview, concentration should be directed to the beginning and end of paragraphs, sections, chapters, and even whole texts, because information tends to be concentrated at the beginning and end of written material.

If you are studying a short academic paper or a complex study book, the Summary, Results and Conclusion sections should always be read first. These sections often include exactly those essences of information for which you are searching, enabling you to grasp that essence without having to wade through a lot of time-wasting material.

Having gained the essence from these sections, simply check that they do indeed summarize the main body of the text.

In the Preview, as with the Overview, you are not fully reading all the material, but simply concentrating once again on special areas.

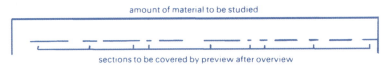

amount of material to be studied

sections to be covered by preview after overview

Sections of a study text to be covered by Preview after Overview.

Strategies for success

The value of this section cannot be overemphasized. A case in point is that of a student taught at Oxford who had spent four months struggling through a 500-page tome on psychology. By the time he had reached page 450 he was beginning to despair because the amount of information he was 'holding on to' as he tried to get to the end was becoming too much – he was literally beginning to drown in the information just before reaching his goal.

It transpired that he had been reading straight through the book, and even though he was nearing the end, did not know what the last chapter was about. It was a complete summary of the book! He read the section and estimated that had he done so at the beginning he would have saved himself approximately 70 hours in reading time, 20 hours in note-taking time and a few hundred hours of worrying.

So in both the Overview and Preview you should very actively select and reject. Many people still feel obliged to read everything in a book even though they know it is not necessarily relevant to them. It is far better to treat a book in the way most people treat lecturers. In other words, if the lecturer is boring, skip what he says, and if he is giving too many examples, is missing the point or is making errors, select, criticize, correct, and disregard as appropriate.

Inview

After the Overview and Preview, and providing that still more information is required, Inview the material. This involves 'filling in' those areas still left, and can be compared with the filling in process of the jigsaw puzzle, once the boundaries and colour areas have been established. It is not necessarily the major reading, as in some cases most of the important material will have been covered in the previous stages.

difficult areas or areas where knowledge not complete

Sections of a study text to be covered after Inview has been completed.

It should be noted from the illustration on page 51 that there are still certain sections that have been left incomplete even at the Inview stage. This is because it is far better to move over particularly difficult points than to batter away at them immediately from one side only.

Once again the comparison with the jigsaw puzzle becomes clear: racking your brains to find the pieces that connect to your 'difficult bit' is a tension-producing waste of time, and jamming the piece in, or cutting it with a pair of scissors so that it does fit (assuming or pretending you understand in context when really you don't), is similarly futile. The difficult sections of a study text are seldom essential to that which follows them, and the advantages of leaving them are manifold:

1   If they are not immediately struggled with, your brain is given that most important brief period in which it can work on them subconsciously. (Most readers will have experienced the examination question which they 'can't possibly answer' only to find on returning to the question later that the answer pops out and often seems ridiculously simple.)

2   If the difficult areas are returned to later, they can be approached from both sides. Apart from its obvious advantages, considering the difficult area in context (as with the difficult bit in the jigsaw) also enables your brain's automatic tendency to fill in gaps to work to greater advantage.

'Jumping over' a stumbling block usually enables the reader to go back to it later on with more information from 'the other side'. The block itself is seldom essential for the understanding of that which follows it.

3   Moving on from a difficult area releases the tension and mental floundering that often accompanies the traditional approach.

Looking at the normal historical development of any discipline, it is found that a fairly regular series of small and logically connected steps are interrupted by great leaps forward.

The propounders of these giant new steps have in many cases 'intuited' them (combining left and right cortex functions), and afterwards been met with scorn. Galileo and Einstein are examples. As they then explained their ideas step by step, others gradually and progressively understood, some early in the explanation, and others as the innovator neared his conclusion.

In the same manner in which the innovator jumps over an enormous number of sequential steps, and in the same manner in which those who first realized his conclusions did so, the studier who leaves out small sections of study will be giving a greater range to his natural creative and understanding abilities.

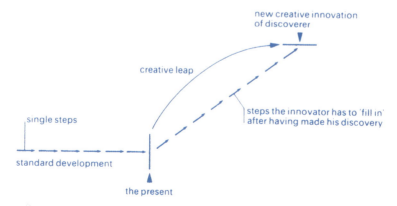

Historical development of ideas and creative innovations.

Review

Having completed the Overview, Preview and Inview, and if further information is still required to complete goals, answer questions or solve problem areas, a Review stage is necessary. In this stage simply fill in all those areas as yet incomplete, and reconsider those sections you marked as noteworthy. In most cases you will find that not much more than 70 per cent of that initially considered relevant will finally be used.

A note on note-taking

Noting while studying should take two main forms:

1   Notes made on the text itself.
2   A growing Mind Map – see Chapter 6.

Notes you make in the textbook itself can include:

1   Underlining.
2   Personal thoughts generated by the text.
3   Critical comments.
4   Marginal straight lines for important or noteworthy material.
5   Curved or wavy marginal lines to indicate unclear or difficult material.
6   Question marks for areas that you wish to research further or that you find questionable.
7   Exclamation marks for outstanding items.
8   Your own symbol code for items and areas that relate to your own specific and general objectives.

Straight line mark for important or noteworthy material.

Curved line mark for difficult or unclear material.

If the textbook is not valuable, markings can be made in colour codes. If the book is a cherished volume, then markings can be made with a very soft pencil. If the pencil is soft enough, and if a very soft eraser is used, the damage to the book will be less than that caused by the finger and thumb as they turn a page.

How to Mind Map this application stage is explained in Chapter 6

Note-taking with Mind Maps®

You will find Mind Mapping the structure of the text as you progress through it a highly accessible study tool and very similar to building up the picture of the jigsaw puzzle as you fit in bit by bit. (To learn how to develop and draw your own Mind Maps for different aspects of study, see Chapters 6 and 7.)

The advantage of building up a Mind Map as you progress through the study text is that you externalize and integrate a lot of information that would otherwise be 'up in the air'. The growing Mind Map also allows you to refer back quickly to areas you have previously covered, rather than having to thumb through pages already read.

It will enable you, after a reasonable amount of basic study, to see just where the areas of confusion in your subject are, and to see also where your subject connects with other subjects. As such it will place you in the creative situation of being able to:

⊙ Integrate the known.

⊙ Realize the relevance to other areas.

⊙ Make appropriate comment where confusion and debate still exist.

The final stage of your study will include the completion and integration of any notes from your text with the Mind Map, which will act as your basis for ongoing study and review.

When you have completed this final stage, you should, as did our imaginary jigsaw puzzle fanatic, celebrate! This may sound humorous, but it is also serious: if you associate the completion of study tasks with personal celebration, the context of your study will become increasingly more pleasant, and thus the probability of your studying far greater.

Once your study programme is well under way, it is advisable to keep enormous 'Master' Mind Maps which summarize and overview the main branches and structures of your subject areas.

See Chapter 6 Mind Maps® for Mind Map® notes

Continuing review

Apart from the immediate review, a continuing review programme is essential, and should be constructed in the light of the knowledge you will find concerning memory (see Chapter 5 on Memory).

We know that memory does not decline immediately after you have learned something, but actually rises before levelling off and then plummeting.

This graph can be warped to your advantage by reviewing just at that point where your memory starts to fall. A review here, at the point of highest memory and integration, will keep the high point up for another one or two days.

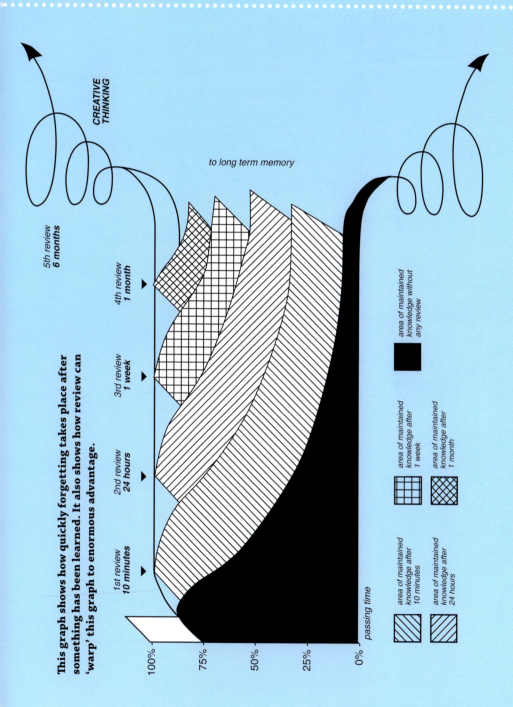

This graph shows how quickly forgetting takes place after something has been learned. It also shows how review can 'warp' this graph to enormous advantage.

CREATIVE THINKING

to long term memory

5th review
6 months

4th review
1 month

3rd review
1 week

2nd review
24 hours

1st review
10 minutes

passing time

100%

75%

50%

25%

0%

area of maintained knowledge without any review

area of maintained knowledge after 1 week

area of maintained knowledge after 1 month

area of maintained knowledge after 10 minutes

area of maintained knowledge after 24 hours

Summary: BOST®

⊙ The entire BOST (Buzan Organic Study Technique) programme must be seen not as a step-by-step progression, but as a series of inter-related aspects of approaching study material. The following three skills-related chapters will impact directly on BOST.

⊙ It is quite possible to switch and change the order from the one given here.

⊙ The amount to be covered may be decided upon before the period of time; the subject matter may be known before the time and amount are decided upon and consequently the knowledge Mind Map could be completed first; the questions can be asked at the preparation stage or after any one of the latter stages; the overview can be eliminated in books where it is inappropriate, or repeated a number of times if the subjects are mathematics or physics. (One student found that it was easier to read four chapters of post-degree mathematics 25 times per week for four weeks quickly, using the survey technique, than to struggle through one formula at a time. He was of course applying to its extreme, but very effectively, the point made about skipping over difficult areas.) Preview can be eliminated or broken down into separate sections; and the Inview and Review can be variously extended or eliminated.

In other words each subject, and each book of each subject, can be confidently approached in the manner best suited to it. To each textbook you will bring the knowledge that, whatever the difficulties, you possess the fundamental understanding to choose the appropriate and necessarily unique approach.

Your study is consequently made a personal, interactive, continually changing and stimulating experience, rather than a rigid, impersonal and tiresomely onerous task.

It should also be noted that although it seems as if the book is being read more times, this is not the case. By using BOST you will be on average reading most sections once only and will then be effectively reviewing those sections considered important. A pictorial representation can be seen below.

'Number of times' book is covered using BOST.

By contrast, the 'once through' reader is *not* reading it once through but is reading it an enormous number of times. He thinks he is reading it through once only because he takes in once piece of information after another. He does not realize that his regressions, back-skipping, re-reading of difficult sentences, general disorganization and forgetting because of inadequate review, result in an actual reading of the book or chapter as many as ten times.

'Number of times' book is covered using traditional 'once through' reading techniques.

Onword

The Buzan Organic Study Technique will allow you easy and effective access to the world of knowledge in a manner that will encourage your brain to learn more and more easily as it learns more, and will turn you from a reluctant learner into one who will avidly devour books by the hundred! The following chapters show you how to **incorporate Speed Reading, Memory** and **Mind Maps** into **BOST**.

4 SPEED READING

The skill of speed reading – which is a complete process of knowledge assimilation – will revolutionize your ability to prioritize and retain essential study facts and figures.

Speed reading will improve your study capabilities. Learning how to do it successfully will:
- Increase your reading speeds dramatically.
- Improve your levels of concentration and comprehension.
- Increase your understanding of how your eyes and brain work.
- Improve your vocabulary and general knowledge.
- Save you time and build your confidence.

The problems to overcome are:
- Deciding what to read: the art of selection.
- Understanding what you read: effective note taking and comprehension.
- **Retaining** information: how to remember what you want to know.
- **Recalling** information: having the ability to recall, on demand, the facts you want and having them at your fingertips.

The study techniques that you will learn in this chapter include:
- Self-assessment: how fast do you read?
- Guided reading techniques that will help you to take in more information more quickly from the written page.
- Tips on how to turn reading problems to your advantage.
- Guidance on how to:
    - Concentrate better.
    - Understand more.

- Scan and skim information to get to the crux of the matter.
- Create your environment to work with you.

Once you have learned the basics, we will up the pace with a section that includes guidance on how to increase your vocabulary to include new prefixes, suffices and word roots. This has the potential to increase your vocabulary from 1000 words to 10,000 words with very little effort.

There are many advantages for your brain in learning to speed read:

- Your eyes will work less hard physically, because you will not need to pause as often to absorb the information you are reading.
- The rhythm and flow of the speed reading process will allow you to absorb the meaning of what you are reading with greater ease. (A slower reading pace encourages more scope for pauses, boredom and loss of concentration, which inhibit comprehension and slow down understanding.)

Self-test your reading speed

Why not test your current reading speed right now, before you start following my techniques? It may be helpful at this point to select a book that you will use specifically for assessing your speed reading progress. In that way, as you move through this chapter, you will get a true picture of the progress you are making, day by day and week by week.

To calculate your speed in words per minute, take the following steps:

1 Read for one minute – note your starting and stopping points within the text.

2 Count the number of words on three lines.

3 Divide that number by three to give you the average number of words per line.

4 Count the number of lines read (balancing short lines out).

5 Multiply the average number of words per line by the number of lines you read and divide the total by the number of minutes spent reading; this will give you your reading speed in words per minute (wpm). Expressed as an equation, the formula for working out speed in wpm is:

$$\text{wpm (speed)} = \frac{\text{number of pages read} \times \text{number of words per average page}}{\text{number of minutes spent reading}}$$

If you work with your brain in the ways described, you can't help but learn to speed read, which, as a result, will add immense value to your experience of learning and understanding.

How you read

Have you ever stopped to think about how you read and assimilate information? Before starting to learn speed reading techniques that will allow you to read as many as 1000 words per minute, take a moment to review the following statements.

⊙ Words are read one at a time.

⊙ Reading faster than 500 words per minute is impossible.

⊙ If you read fast you are not able to appreciate what you are reading.

- High reading speeds mean lower levels of concentration.
- Average reading speeds are natural, and therefore the best way to learn.

To which of the following statements would you reply 'True' and to which 'False'?

- Words are read one at a time.

    False – We read for meaning, not for single words.
- Reading faster than 500 words per minute is impossible.

    False – We have the capacity to take in as many as six words at a time and as many as twenty-four words a second.
- If you read fast you are not able to appreciate what you are reading.

    False – The faster reader will understand more of what is being expressed, will experience greater levels of concentration and will have time to review areas of special interest and relevance.
- High reading speeds mean lower levels of concentration.

    False – The faster we read, the more impetus we gather and the more we concentrate.
- Average reading speeds are natural, and therefore the best way to learn.

    False – Average reading speeds are *not* natural; they are simply the result of the limitations of the way we were taught to read.

Changing a personal belief about what is possible will help you to understand the process of speed reading; it will also encourage your success because your mind will not be hindering your progress with the weight of false assumptions.

Guided eye movements

If I were to sit with you as you read this study guide and ask you to show me with your forefinger how you believe your eyes move across the page, what do you think the speed and path of that movement would look like? The majority of people would trace each line of text in straight lines from left to right, as they move gradually down the page. However, they would be incorrect.

Stop-start sweeps

The average reader takes in approximately 200–240 words per minute. Taking in text line by line is an effective way to absorb information, but it is not the fastest. There are many different pathways by which our eyes can travel across a page and still successfully absorb information.

When we read, our eyes actually make small and regular 'jumps', pausing or 'fixating' in order to take in information (see illustration on page 70). Your eyes therefore do not move smoothly in one continuous sweep across the page; they stop and start in order to take in information. It is possible to make an immediate improvement in your reading speed by spending less time on each pause, and but using a guide such as a pencil. Interestingly, the eyes can see things clearly only when they can 'hold them still':

⊙ If an object is still, your eyes must be still in order to see it.
⊙ If an object is moving, your eyes must move with the object in order to see it.

Test this for yourself by holding a finger in front of your eyes. When it is still, your eyes are still; when it moves, your eyes follow it in order to see it. In relation to reading, this means that your eyes have to pause to take in the words, because the words are static. This is a critical speed reading concept. When your eyes pause, they can take in up to five or six words at a time. They can easily fixate after the beginning and before the end of the line, thus taking in the information 'to the side'.

If you use a visual aid, it minimizes the amount of work that your eyes have to do, keeps your brain focused and maintains constant reading speeds, combined with high levels of understanding.

Take a look at the diagrams on the next page.

Figure (B) shows what happens in the eye movements of a poor reader. This reader pauses or fixates on words for twice as long as most people. Extra pauses are caused because the reader often re-reads words, sometimes skipping back in as many as three places to make sure that the correct meaning has been taken in. Research has shown that, in 80 per cent of cases when readers were not allowed to skip back or regress, they had taken in all the necessary information.

Figure (C) shows that the good reader, while not back-skipping or regressing, also has longer jumps between groups of words.

On a normal page of 12 words per line, the weaker reader will fixate on single words, back-skip and regress while reading, pausing approximately 14 times, for an average of half a second per pause. That's a time of seven seconds per line. A speed reader, on the other hand, with minor adjustments and no interruptions, would take no more than two seconds per line.

The techniques that follow are designed to overcome the common problems of back-skipping, visual wandering and regression that impede progress and will instead lead you towards taking in more and more words each time your eyes fixate on the page, as in Figure (C).

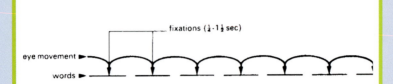

Figure A: Diagram representing the stop-and-start movement or 'jumps' of the eyes during the reading process.

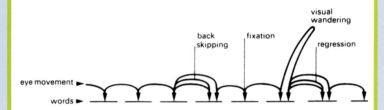

Figure B: Diagram showing poor reading habits of a slow reader: one word read at a time, with unconscious back-skipping, visual wanderings and conscious regressions.

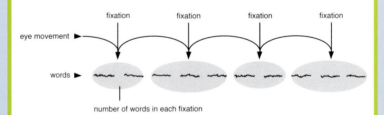

Figure C: Diagram showing eye movements of a better and more efficient reader. More words are taken in at each fixation, and back-skipping, regression and visual wandering are reduced.

Seven steps to speed up your reading

Reading is usually described as 'getting from a book what the author intended' or, 'assimilating the facts, figures and theories'; but I believe it to be more than that: **reading is the individual's total interrelationship with symbolic information.**

At its core is a process taking place on many different levels at the same time – and it is usually related to the visual aspect of learning, that is, what we can see. For reading to be informative and for reading methods to be effective, the following seven levels of understanding need to be absorbed. Every level must be further developed if you are to become an effective speed reader.

1 Recognition.
2 Assimilation.
3 Comprehension.
4 Knowledge.
5 Retention.
6 Recall.
7 Communication.

Recognition

Your knowledge of the alphabetic symbols. This step takes place before the physical aspect of reading begins.

Assimilation

The physical process by which light is reflected from the word and is received by the eye. It is then transmitted via the optic nerve to your brain.

Comprehension

The linking together of all parts of the information being read with all other appropriate information. This includes words, figures, concepts, facts and pictures. (I call this 'intra-integration'.)

Knowledge

The process by which you bring the whole body of your previous knowledge to the new information that you are reading, whilst making the appropriate connections. This includes analysis, criticism, appreciation, selection and rejection of information. (I call this 'extra-integration'.)

Retention

The basic storage of information. Storage can itself become a problem; most students will have experienced the anxiety of being in an examination and having trouble retrieving some of that essential information successfully. Storage on its own is not enough – it must be accompanied by 'recall'.

Recall

Critically, the ability to retrieve from storage the information that is needed, ideally *when* it is needed.

Communication

The use to which the acquired information is immediately or eventually put: in your case essays, written and oral examinations and creative manifestations. Most significantly, communication also includes that all-important function; thinking.

Now that you have understood the full definition of reading and its application to speeding up your reading, we can move on to dealing with some major reading problems.

Beat reading 'problems'

'Once a problem is faced, analyzed and understood it becomes a positive energy centre for the creation of solutions.'

Many of us hold false beliefs about reading and our ability to read. Take a moment to think about what you consider to be your problems with reading – the most commonly experienced being:

Vision   **Speed**   **Comprehension**   **Time**
Amount   **Noting**   **Retention**   **Fear**   **Recall**
Fatigue   **Boredom**   **Analysis**   **Organization**
Vocabulary   **Selection**   **Rejection**
Concentration

These traits are not the result of lack of ability, but of negative self-belief, inappropriate teaching methods, or a lack of understanding about how your eyes and brain work together to assimilate information.

Four common reading 'problems' that with a change of perspective are positively *beneficial* to learning speed reading are:

sub-vocalization
finger-pointing
regression
back-skipping

Sub-vocalization

The tendency to 'mouth' words as you are reading is known as sub-vocalization. It is a natural stage in learning to read. It could be a barrier to learning to speed read for some people if they were dependent upon it for understanding, because it may slow down the rate at which words are read. However, as it is quite possible for your brain to sub-vocalize 2000 words per minute, the problem vanishes!

The *advantage* of sub-vocalization is that it can reinforce what is being read. You can choose to use your inner voice selectively – to emphasize important words or concepts – by increasing the volume on demand and literally shouting them out internally. The technique then becomes a positive memory aid.

Sub-vocalization can be of positive benefit to dyslexic readers, because internalizing the sound of the words as they are read will provide a reminder of the shape of the individual letters and will appeal to both the right and left sides of the brain.

Finger-pointing

Most people find that they are more comfortable having a guide to follow, which makes their eyes far more relaxed and efficient. This is because the eyes are designed to follow movement. Far from being a disadvantage, finger-pointing can actually help in learning to speed read. I would simply recommend that you may prefer to use a slimmer, purpose-designed reading aid, since fingers can be large and bulky and may obscure some words.

Regression and back-skipping

Regression is the conscious process of returning to words, phrases or paragraphs that you feel you must have missed or misunderstood.

Back-skipping is a similar but unconscious process of re-reading material that has just been read.

Although regression and back-skipping are slightly different traits, they both are related to a lack of confidence and a tendency to stay in a reading 'comfort zone'. They are habits that can be altered.

Re-reading material has been shown to make no difference to levels of understanding, so all you are doing is putting added pressure on your eyes. The simplest way to force yourself to break these habits is to increase your reading speed, and to maintain a rhythm as you read.

Your amazing eyes

Each of your eyes is an amazing optical instrument, far superior in its precision and complexity to the most advanced telescope or microscope. We have known for some time that our pupils adjust their size according to the intensity of light and the nearness of the object viewed. The brighter the light and the nearer the object, the smaller the size of the pupil (of the eye, that is!).

We also know that pupil size adjusts in tune with emotion, so if, for example, you are gazing at someone you are attracted to, your pupil size will increase automatically. This means that the more you can generate and maintain interest in your subject, the easier it will be for you to absorb the information you are needing.

How do your eyes 'read' information?

The retina at the back of the eye is a light receiver. When your eye takes in a range of complex images, the retinal light receivers decode the images and send them along the optic nerve to the visual area of your brain, known as the occipital lobe.

The occipital lobe is located not behind the eyes, but at the back of your head; so the popular phrase is correct; we really do have eyes 'in the back of the head'.

Your occipital lobe directs your eyes around the page to hunt for information that is of interest. This knowledge forms the basis of the revolutionary approach to speed reading that is explained here.

Exercises to increase your 'mind's eye'

The next series of exercises is designed to expand your visual power so that you are able to take in more words 'at a glance' when you look at a page.

Measuring your horizontal and vertical vision

Read through these instructions once first before trying the technique or, alternatively, ask a fellow student to read the passage to you while you follow the directions:

Look straight ahead and focus your attention on a point on the horizon as far away as possible, then:

⊙ Touch the tips of your two forefingers together so they form a horizontal line, then hold them approximately 10 cm (4 inches) in front of your nose.

⊙ While keeping your eyes fixed on your chosen point in the distance, begin to wiggle the tips of your fingers and move them apart slowly, along a straight, horizontal line. (You will need to move your arms and elbows apart as well, but keep the movement horizontal.)

⊙ Keep going until your fingers move just outside your field of vision and you can no longer see the movement of your fingers out of the corner of your eyes.

⊙ Stop and ask your friend to measure how far apart your fingers are.

Now repeat the exercise, but with one forefinger pointing upwards and the other downwards, so that the fingertips meet in a vertical line this time. Again, hold them together, approximately 10 cm (4 in) in front of your nose.

⊙ While keeping your eyes fixed firmly on your chosen point in the distance, begin to wiggle your fingers and move them apart – one upwards, one downwards – in a vertical line so that they gradually move out of the top and bottom of your field of vision.

⊙ Stop and measure how far apart your fingers are.

Does it surprise you to find out just how much and how far you can see when you are apparently focused solely on something else? How is this possible?

The answer lies in the unique design of the human eye. Each of your eyes has 130 million light receivers in its retina, which means that you have 260 million receivers of light in total. Your central focus (that part which you use to read your book, or focus on the point in the distance) takes up only 20 per cent of this light-receiving capacity. The rest – that is 80 per cent of the total light receivers – are devoted to your peripheral vision.

By learning to make greater use of your peripheral vision while you are reading, you will begin to utilize the vast untapped potential of your peripheral vision: your mind's eye.

What do I mean by the 'mind's eye'? I mean the ability to read or see with your entire brain, not just with your eyes. It is a concept that is recognized by those who practise yoga, meditation or prayer and by anyone familiar with learning to 'see' Magic Eye™ three-dimensional pictures.

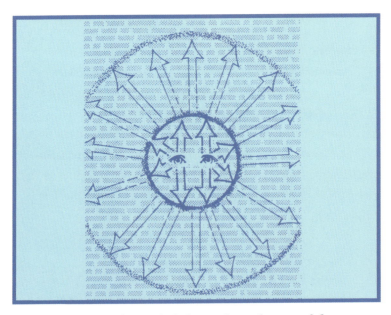

Fields of vision. The inner circled area shows the area of clear vision available to the speed reader when the eye/brain system is used properly. The outer circle shows the peripheral vision also available.

See with your mind's eye

When you have read through the guidelines of the following exercise, turn to page 83 and place your finger directly underneath the word 'Daydreaming' in the middle of the page. Keeping your eyes totally focused on that central word, and without moving them:

⊙ See how many words you can observe to either side of the central word.

⊙ See how many words you can make out clearly above and below the word at which you are pointing.

⊙ See if you can tell whether there is a number at the top or the bottom of the page and, if so, what that number is.

⊙ See whether you can count the number of images on the opposite page.

⊙ See whether you can count the number of paragraphs on the opposite page.

⊙ Can you determine clearly or roughly what the image on the opposite page is illustrating?

Most people answer 'yes' to the majority of these questions, which shows that most people have the innate capacity to read using their peripheral vision as well as their central vision. By this means, you use all 260 million of your eye's light receivers to communicate with and illuminate your brain.

This revolutionary new approach means that, from now on, you will read with your brain and not just with your eyes. The image opposite shows clearly the two levels of vision that are available. The inner circle of vision is the one with which we are all familiar; the outer circle shows the field of peripheral vision that is available to us, if we choose to use it.

Reading bites

⊙ If you are able to combine peripheral vision with central focus you will be able to see and absorb information from entire paragraphs and pages at the same time.

⊙ You can expand your peripheral vision by holding your textbook further away from your eyes than usual. It will enable your peripheral vision to work better.

⊙ While your central focus is taking in the detail line by line, your peripheral vision is able to review what has been read and assess the value of what is to come.

⊙ This practice is also easier on the eyes, as they do not need to over-work their muscles.

> **Remember: it is your brain that reads – your eyes are just the very sophisticated lenses that it uses to do so.**

Three key guided reading techniques

Open this book (or any book) at any page, and look at it for one second only. Do you think you could recognize the same page again? The answer is 'yes'. If you doubt the truth of this, think of how much information your eyes can take in and your brain can remember in a fraction of a second when on the road, at a railway station, or anywhere where you are seeing a multitude of different images and influences at the same time. Think how few images are on a page of text in comparison.

The three key reading techniques that follow are designed to super-power your vision.

First practise each technique at a very high reading speed – without pausing or worrying about whether or not you understand what you are reading.

Then practise each technique at normal speed.

In this way your brain will gradually become accustomed to your faster reading speeds. (You may find it useful to begin by re-reading familiar material, so you have the benefit of reviewing something that you already know, while 'warming up' your brain for the tasks ahead.)

1 The double-line sweep

involves your eyes taking in two lines of text at a time. It is a technique that combines both vertical and horizontal vision (and a skill applied by those studying music).

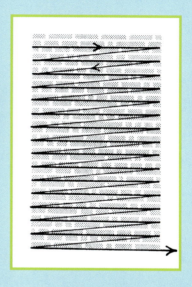

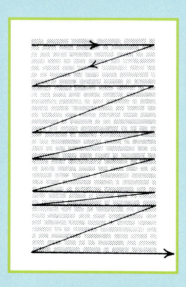

2 The variable sweep takes

the same approach as the double-line sweep, but allows you to take in the number of lines that you can cope with at one time.

3 **The reverse sweep** is identical to the previous two but with one significant difference: you are altering the process to review each section of text in reverse. This may sound absurd, but it makes sense if you recall that the eye can take in information only by fixing attention, and that words are viewed in groups of five or six.

In reading backwards you are simply 'holding' all the information you have in your mind, until you receive the final piece of the jigsaw at the start of each line. This has the benefit of enabling you to review the text at the same time as reading it – which will speed up your reading and improve your levels of concentration and comprehension.

Each of these 'sweep' techniques can be used for
- Previewing.
- Skimming.
- Scanning.

for information, and you can take in as many lines as you choose. You can shorten (by taking in fewer lines) or lengthen (by taking in more lines) your sweeps, or combine more than one technique. This applies specifically to the Preparation and Overview sections in BOST.

Supercharge your speed reading

Now it's time to explore and improve your:

1   Powers of concentration.
2   Ability to scan and skim data.
3   Environmental influences on studying.

Improving concentration

In my experience of teaching and lecturing around the world, I have found that the vast majority of people believe that they suffer from regular periods of poor concentration. Many people say that they find themselves daydreaming instead of applying themselves to the task in hand. In fact, this is good news and is perfectly natural. Daydreaming occurs naturally every few minutes and it is your brain's way of taking a break in order to absorb what it has learnt.

If you think about it, you have not actually lost concentration, you have just chosen to concentrate on a series of other points of interest instead: the cat on the chair; the mobile ring tones; a sample of music on the radio; or someone walking along the street – to name but a few distractions.

> **The problem is not your powers of concentration, it is the direction and focus of that concentration.**

When you master the art of concentration, your entire eye-brain system becomes laser-like, with an extraordinary ability to focus and absorb information.

Causes of poor concentration

1   Vocabulary difficulties

Efficient and concentrated speed reading relies upon a smooth flow of information with few interruptions in understanding. Pauses to look up words or to ponder will break your concentration and slow your understanding of the whole. If you come across a word that you don't understand when reading, rather than looking it up straight away, underline it and review it afterwards.

2   Conceptual difficulties

If you don't really understand the concepts you are reading about you will have difficulty concentrating. To get past this obstacle, choose one of the guiding techniques outlined on page 80 and use skimming and scanning as ways of multiple-reading the material until it becomes familiar to you.

3   Inappropriate reading speed

Many people believe (because that is what they were taught) that reading things slowly and carefully will help understanding and comprehension. This approach is actually counter-productive and, far from aiding your brain, reading slowly will actually slow it down. To check this out, try reading the following statement exactly as it is laid out. Read it 'slowly and carefully':

Speed read ing has be en found to be bet ter for understand ing than slow read ing.

You probably found that hard work because your brain is not designed to take in information at such a slow pace. If you skim read it fast, the words will make instant sense. Now read the following sentence, this time reading the words as they are grouped:

It has been discovered   that the human brain with the help   of its eyes   takes in information far more easily   when the information is conveniently grouped   in meaningful bundles.

An increase in the speed of reading leads to an automatic increase in comprehension. If you apply the speed reading techniques outlined in this book, your brain will develop the capacity to organize words into meaningful groups as you read.

> **Reading slowly and carefully encourages your brain to read more and more slowly, with less and less comprehension.**

4   Distraction

Another common enemy of concentration is allowing your mind to remain focused on something else, instead of the task in hand. For example, you may need to finish reading a primary reference for a tutorial tomorrow morning, but your mind keeps wandering to your mates, to the disagreement you had with your partner, to money worries, to the gig you are all going to tomorrow.

If you find yourself getting easily distracted, you will need to 'shake off' the threads of thought that are diverting you by refocusing on what you are trying to achieve. You may even want to stop for a moment to Mind Map your current aims to help you gather your thoughts.

5   Poor organization

Sitting down to read something can sometimes feel like a personal battle. Having begun to read, the distractions begin: you have no pencil, cup of coffee, notepaper or spectacles... Constant distractions make it harder to build the impetus to begin again. The answer is simple: plan ahead so that you have everything you need close to hand, set yourself achievement targets and plan your breaks to coincide with completion of those tasks.

6   Lack of interest

An apparent lack of interest is often linked to other difficulties. For example: confusing material, lack of specialist vocabulary, conflicting priorities, negative attitude and other obstacles to concentration that are listed above. It is worth trying to solve these related issues first and then, if necessary, apply the 'harsh critic' approach.

Get annoyed with the material you are trying to read. In that way you will be drawn in, in the way you would to a debate with someone whose opinions you oppose.

7   Lack of motivation

Lack of motivation relates to a lack of goal. If you don't know why you are reading a study text it can be hard to motivate yourself to be interested in reading it.

Review your goals. It's an obvious thing to say, but once you become clear about why you need to absorb the information you will be better able to complete the task. Use organization and personal interest to realign yourself with your target, and use your preferred guided reading technique to ensure that you complete the task as quickly as possible – and with optimum return.

Use scanning and skimming

Scanning and skimming are designed to combine your recently acquired skill of guided reading with special emphasis on the way your brain can pre-select information automatically (*your mental set*).

Scanning is a natural skill. You use it when you are scanning a crowd for a face that you know, or when you are scanning a road sign for relevant directions. You use scanning when the eye glances over a range of material to find a very specific piece of information – usually in the context of text when you need to look up a particular piece of information in a book or lecture notes, or a relevant link on a website.

As long as you know what you are looking for in advance and understand how the information is organized (for example, in alphabetical order or by theme), then this technique is simple. If you want to find particular information, use scanning.

Skimming is a more complex method than scanning and is similar to the guided reading skill explained earlier. It is used to gain a general overview of information so that the 'bricks and mortar', the framework of the content, rather than the detailed rooms and furnishings are understood.

Efficient skim reading can be done at speeds of 1000 words per minute or more, while still gaining an outline understanding of what is being said. If you want to acquire a general overview of material, use skimming.

Environmental influences

Without doubt:

- Your environment – your posture and place of study – will affect your level of achievement.
- Your sense of physical well-being will influence your ability to take in information.

If you are feeling negative or unwell, or your study area is crammed or cluttered, your state of being will have a negative influence on your productivity. If, on the other hand, you are happy in your environment and inwardly content, you will react positively to reading and will comprehend new information better. It therefore makes sense to ensure that your environment is as positive and conducive to study as possible.

Placement and intensity of light

Whenever possible, it is best to study in natural daylight. Indeed, a recent study found that exposing yourself to daylight allows your brain to release more 'good guy' hormones, so your desk or tabletop should ideally be placed near a window. At other times, artificial light should come over your shoulder, opposite the hand with which you write. The lamp should be bright enough to illuminate the material being read, but not so bright that it provides a contrast with the rest of the room. If you are using a desktop or laptop computer, then the screen should be facing toward, not away from, the light.

All study materials at hand

To enable your brain to work comfortably and in a focused way, it is useful to have all the work materials and reference guides that you might need placed easily to hand. It will help you feel prepared and relaxed and better able to concentrate on the task.

Height of chair and desk

Making yourself too comfortable is counter-productive, because you will be tempted to fall asleep instead of concentrate! Ideally, your chair should be upright, with a straight back, and neither too hard nor too soft. Swivel and office chairs especially should support you comfortably, ensuring good posture. The chair should be adjustable and high enough to allow your thighs to be parallel with the floor, because your sitting bones will then be taking the strain. The desk should be approximately 20 cm (8 inches) above the seat of the chair. 'Kneel', 'kneeling' or 'posture' chairs are a very good medium for study as they encourage correct posture.

Distance of the eyes from the reading material

The natural distance for your eyes from your reading material is approximately 50 cm (20 in). This makes it easier for your eyes to focus on groups of words and lessens the possibility of eye strain or headaches.

Your posture

Ideally your feet should be flat on the floor, your back upright, with the slight curve in your back maintained to give you support. If you sit up either too 'straight' or slumped, you will exhaust yourself and strain your back. Try either holding the book, or resting it on something so that it is slightly upright, rather than flat.

Sitting correctly has a number of physiological benefits for studying:

⊙ Your brain receives the maximum flow of air and blood because your windpipe, veins and arteries are functioning unrestricted.

⊙ It optimizes the flow of energy up your spine and maximizes the power of your brain.

⊙ If your body is alert then your brain knows something important is happening (conversely, if you sit in a slumped position, you are telling your brain that it is time to sleep!).

⊙ Your eyes can make full use of both your central and peripheral vision.

Finding your optimum studying time

We all have peaks and troughs of concentration and each of us is likely to find that we read or concentrate best at different times of the day. There are 'larks' who work best between 5 a.m. and 9 a.m.; 'owls' who are at their most productive in the evening and at night; and others who find that late morning or early afternoon suits them best, though periods immediately before or after eating allow hunger and drowsiness respectively to interfere with concentration. You may not know what is your optimum time, so experiment with working at different times of day – see what works best for you; it may alter dramatically your propensity to concentrate on study.

Minimize interruptions

It is as important to minimize external interruptions when you are reading as it is to minimize the pauses while you read. External interruptions, such as telephone calls or personal diversions (for instance, unnecessary breaks), are the enemy of concentration and focus. Similarly, if you are worrying about something personal or are in physical discomfort, your preoccupation with other influences will reduce your concentration and comprehension.

So divert your phone to voicemail, play music that will help you concentrate and keep your area free of distractions and temptations. (And turn your computer off, if you are not using it, so that you are not tempted onto the Internet.)

Mastermind your vocabulary

Vocabulary is important for many reasons. The person with a broad vocabulary is at a greater advantage when it comes to study.

Most of us have more than one vocabulary, and usually we have at least three. These are:

- The vocabulary we use in conversation.
- The vocabulary we use when writing.
- The vocabulary of word recognition.

DID YOU KNOW?

- The average person's spoken vocabulary is about 1000 words.
- The number of available words is over 3,000,000.
- Improving your vocabulary raises your intelligence.

Our conversational vocabulary tends to be limited to a maximum of 1000 words per person; our written vocabulary is greater because we take more care over our choice of words and sentence structure when we are drafting text; but the largest of the three is our recognition vocabulary. We understand many more words than we use.

In theory our conversational vocabulary should be as large as our recognition vocabulary, but that is rarely the case. It is possible, however, to increase the size of all three quite dramatically – and therefore your speed reading capabilities.

The next three sections will explore the word power of prefixes, suffixes and word roots. They are powerful shortcuts to increasing your language and vocabulary.

The power of prefixes

Prefixes are letters, syllables or words placed at the beginning of a word that alter meaning. Learning just a few prefixes will expand your vocabulary enormously. Many of them are concerned with position, opposition and movement. *They are mini words with power.*

The list of prefixes following is a selection of some of the most common ones; these were found within over 14,000 words from a standard desktop dictionary.

You will increase your potential vocabulary instantly by at least 10,000 words if you are able to remember and use these prefixes, by adding them to the beginning of words. Be on the lookout for them as you read from now on.

Words containing key prefixes

Word	Prefix	Common meaning	Root	Common meaning
precept	*pre-*	before	*capere*	take, seize
detain	*de-*	away, down	*tenere*	hold, have
intermittent	*inter-*	between, among	*mittere*	send
offer	*ob-*	against	*ferre*	bear, carry
insist	*in-*	into	*stare*	stand
monograph	*mono-*	alone, one	*graphein*	write
epilogue	*epi-*	upon	*logos*	speech, study of
advance	*ad-*	to, toward	*specere*	see
uncomplicated	*un-* *com-*	not together with	*plicare*	fold
non-extended	*non-* *ex-*	not out, beyond	*tender*	stretch
reproduction	*re-* *pro-*	back, again forward, for	*ducere*	lead
indisposed	*in-* *dis-*	not apart, not	*ponere*	put, place
over-sufficient	*over-* *sub-*	above under	*facere*	make, do
mistranscribe	*mis-* *trans-*	wrong across, beyond	*scribere*	write

Eye-cue vocabulary exercise – prefixes

Choose five words from the following list of six, to complete sentences 1–5 accurately:

Examinations   **Reviewing**   **Comprehension**
Prepare   **Depress**   **Progress**

1   In order to be ready for a meeting or other event it is always best to .... in advance.

2   .... what you have learned will help to consolidate the associations in your memory.

3   Negative thoughts .... the brain and inhibit your ability to remember effectively.

4   Speed reading improves reading efficiency as well as

....

5   Preparing for .... needn't be daunting if you use speed reading and Mind Maps as your memory tools.

Now refer to page 190 for the answers.

Fourteen suffixes

G = Greek, L = Latin, F = French, E = English

Suffix	Meaning	Example
-able, -ible (L)	capable of, fit for	durable, comprehensible
-al, -ail (L)	relating to quality	abdominal
-ance, -ence,	or action of forming	
-ant (L)	adjectives of quality,	insurance,
	nouns signifying	corpulence
	a personal agent or	defiant, servant
	something	
	producing an effect	
-ation, -ition (L)	action or state of	condition, dilapidation
-er (E)	belonging to	farmer, New Yorker
-ism (E)	quality or doctrine of	realism, socialism
-ive (L)	nature of	creative, receptive
-ize, -ise (G)	make, practise, act like	modernize, advertise
-logy (G)	indicating a branch of knowledge	biology, psychology
-ly (E)	having the quality of	softly, quickly
-or (L)	a state or action, a person who, or thing which	victor, generator
-ous, -ose (L)	full of	murderous, anxious, officious, morose
-some	like	gladsome
-y (E)	condition	difficulty

The strength of suffixes

Suffixes are letters, syllables or words that are placed at the end of a word to alter meaning. They are often concerned with characteristics or qualities of something, or with changing from one part of speech to another (for example, from adjectives into verbs).

Eye-cue vocabulary exercise – suffixes

Choose five words from the following list of six, to complete sentences 1–5 accurately:

Minimal	**Winsome**	**Psychology**
Vociferous	**Hedonism**	**Practitioner**

1 A .... is one who works in a certain field, such as medicine.

2 The doctrine of pursuing pleasure as the highest good is known as ....

3 A charge for something which relates to the lowest or smallest price is ....

4 People who speak loudly and often are ....

5 The branch of knowledge that deals with the human mind and its functioning is known as ....

Now refer to page 190 for the answers.

An A–Z of roots

This is the final section to focus on developing vocabulary and following is a list of 14 Latin and Greek root words that are commonly used in modern English.

Fourteen roots

Root	Meaning	Example
aer	air	aerate, aeroplane
am (from *amare*)	love	amorous, amateur, amiable
chron	time	chronology, chronic
dic, dict	say, speak	dictate
equi	equal	equidistant
graph	write	calligraphy, graphology, telegraph
luc (from *lux*)	light	elucidate
pot, poss, poten (from *ponerte*)	be able	potential, possible
quaerere	ask, seek	question, inquiry, query
sent, sens (from *sentire*)	feel	sensitive, sentient
soph	wise	philosopher
spect (from *spicere*)	look	introspective, inspect
spir (from *spirare*)	breathe	inspiration
vid, vis (from *videre*)	see	supervisor, vision, provident

Eye-cue vocabulary exercise – roots

Choose five words from the following list of six, to complete sentences 1–5 accurately:

Aerodynamics   **Equinox**   **Egocentric**
Querulous   **Chronometer**   **Amiable**

1   A person who is quarrelsome and discontented, and who complains in a questioning manner is ....

2   A person who is friendly and lovable is often described as ....

3   The .... is that time of year when both day and night are of equal length.

4   An instrument that finely measures time is a ....

5   The science which deals with the forces exerted by air and by gaseous fluids is ....

Now refer to page 190 for the answers.

How to use prefixes, suffixes and roots

The first time you look over these lists many of the words will seem unfamiliar, and getting to know them may feel daunting. In order to make the words more familiar and to help them become part of your daily vocabulary, I would like to offer the following tips:

⊙ Browse through a good dictionary, and become familiar with the various ways in which these suffixes, prefixes and root words are used.

⊙ Keep a record of Key Words and phrases that stand out for you and are useful in some way.

⊙ Commit to making an effort to introduce one new word into your vocabulary each day. New words, like any information, need to be repeated a minimum of five times over an extended period before they become a permanent feature of your memory.

⊙ Listen for new and exciting words in conversation that you want to make a part of your growing vocabulary – and don't be shy about making a note of what you hear.

⊙ Make a mental note to look up words that you don't understand when you read a study text; wait until you have finished reading the chapter, passage or paper. Don't interrupt the flow of what you are doing.

If you consciously improve your vocabulary by adding a few words and phrases each day, you will also improve your overall intellect as well as your general understanding and comprehension.

At the same time your speed reading ability will accelerate because of your increased ability to spot Key Words and concepts, and you will have fewer problems understanding what you are reading.

In addition, you will no longer be tempted to back-skip as you read because you will have the confidence to know that your vocabulary is broad enough to support your general comprehension.

Onword

You are now equipped to be a super-fast Study Reader. In the next chapter, you will learn how to remember what you have speed read.

5 SUPERCHARGE YOUR MEMORY

How good are you at remembering facts and figures? Are you worried about recalling information under pressure in exams? This chapter provides you with easy-to-follow memory techniques and exercises to enable you to develop a supercharged memory, and will help you to overcome poor information retention by utilizing the memory enhancement method of Mind Mapping.

We've noted in Chapter 1 how data and information are taken in by your brain and stored in your memory in many different ways and are processed by either:

⊙ The right side of your brain – concerned with rhythm, imagination, daydreaming, colour, dimension, spatial awareness, completeness.

⊙ The left side of your brain – concerned with logic, words, lists, numbers, sequence, lines, analysis.

To recap, we also know the two sides of your brain do not operate separately – they need to work together to be at their most effective. The more you can stimulate both sides of your brain at the same time, the more effectively they will work together to help you to think better, remember more, and recall instantly.

Helping your brain to learn

A memory system works rather like a super-sized filing cabinet that contains files on every aspect of your entire life. The only way you are going to find information quickly and easily in your cabinet is to make sure that it is

⊙ Well organized.

⊙ Accessible.

This means that no matter how obscure the memory you want to retrieve, you know what its category is and can find it easily.

In order to be able to categorize and store the information in the filing cabinet that is your memory, it is important to have some understanding of how your brain and memory function while you are learning.

Research has shown that first and last impressions matter to your brain. In every situation, we are more likely to remember things that happen or that are introduced:

- At the beginning – the Primacy Effect.
- At the end – the Recency Effect.

We also find it easier to remember things that are:

- Associated with items or thoughts that are already stored in the memory.
- Outstanding or unique – as this appeals to the imagination.

Your brain is more likely to notice and recall something that has strong appeal:

- To your senses – taste, smell, touch, sound or sight.
- To your particular interests.

Your brain is geared to create patterns and maps, and to finish sequences; which is why, if a familiar song on the radio stops halfway through, you will probably keep humming it to completion; or if a sequence of paragraphs is numbered one to six and point three is missing, you will search for the missing point three.

Your brain also needs help to remember facts, figures, and other important reference information that needs to be bought quickly to mind. An aid that assists memory is a mnemonic.

Mnemonics

A mnemonic may be a word, a picture, a system or other device that will help you to recall a phrase, a name or a sequence of facts. The 'm' in mnemonic is silent (it is pronounced 'nem-on-ic') and the word comes from the Greek word *mnemon*, which means 'mindful'.

Most of us will have used mnemonic techniques during our schooldays, even if we didn't realize it at the time. Students learning music are often taught the phrase '**E**very **G**ood **B**oy **D**eserves **F**avour' to help them remember the notes **EGBDF**.

Many of us will have learned the poem 'Thirty days hath September, April, June and November...' to help remember which months have 30 days and which have 31 ('except for February, alone...'). That too is a mnemonic: a device to help you to remember.

Mnemonics work by stimulating your imagination, and by using words and other tools to encourage your brain to make associations.

Key misconceptions

⊙ As people get older, they often think that their memory is fading. This is false thinking.

⊙ Those who are working under stress may find recalling information a challenge and feel they will never be able to hold anything in their mind for long ever again. However, this is more to do with not giving yourself time to pause and think, and having poor methods of recall.

Your memory is highly effective – although your process of recalling information may not be as effective as you'd like it to be. You need only to refine the way you access the information that is stored in your brain. To begin the process, try this simple exercise.

Word recall exercise 1

Below is a list of words. Read each word on this list once, quickly, in order. Then turn to page 108, and fill in as many of the words as you can. Unless you are a grandmaster of memory, you will not be able to remember all of them, so simply try for as many as possible.

    Then read the complete list again, one word after the other. To ensure you do this properly, use a small card, covering each word as you read it.

    When you have finished, turn back to page 108 to answer a few questions that will show you how your memory works.

house	rope
floor	watch
wall	Shakespeare
glass	ring
roof	and
tree	of
sky	the
road	table
the	pen
of	flower
and	pain
of	dog
and	

Now fill in as many of the words, in order, as you can, without referring to the original list.

_____   _____

_____   _____

_____   _____

_____   _____

_____   _____

_____   _____

_____   _____

_____   _____

_____   _____

_____   _____

Recall during learning

⦿ How many words from the beginning of the list did you remember?

⦿ How many words from the end of the list did you remember?

⦿ Did you recall any words that appeared more than once?

⦿ Were there any words in the list that stood out in your memory as outstandingly different?

⦿ How many words from the middle of the list did you remember (that you have not already noted)?

In this test almost everyone recalls similar information:

⦿ One to seven words from the beginning of the list.

- One or two words from the end of the list.
- Most of the words that appear more than once (in this case: the, and, of).
- The outstanding word or phrase (in this case: Shakespeare).
- Relatively few, if any, words from the middle of the list.

Why should this similarity occur? This pattern of results shows that **memory** and **understanding** do not work in the same way: although all the words were understood, not all of them were remembered. Our ability to recall information we understand is related to several factors:

- We tend to remember **first things** and **last things** more easily than **things in between**. Therefore we recall more information from the beginning and the end of a learning period. (See how the curve of the graph at the top of page 111 begins high at the start, drops before the three peaks, and lifts again before the end.)

  In the case of the word recall test, the words 'house' and 'dog' appear at the beginning and the end of the sequence.
- We learn more when things are **Associated** or **Linked** in some way: by using rhyme, repetition, or something that connects with our senses. (See points A, B, C on the graph on page 110).

  In the case of the word recall test, repetitive words include: 'the', 'at', 'of', 'and'; associated words are: 'Shakespeare' and 'pen'; or 'house', 'wall' and 'roof'.
- We also learn more when things are Outstanding or Unique. (See point O on the graph on page 110).

The best time period in which we can recall and understand the most has been found to be between **20** and **60 minutes** after

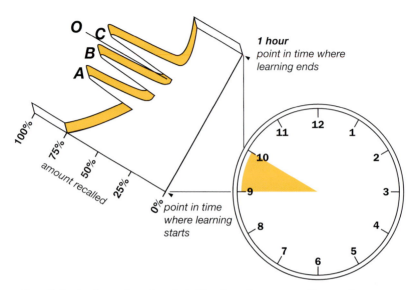

Recall *during* learning. Graph indicating that we recall more from the beginning and ends of a learning period. We also recall more when things are associated or linked (A, B and C) and more when things are outstanding or unique (O).

the starting point. A shorter period does not give your mind long enough to assimilate what is being learned.

This will make sense to those of us studying in a lesson when it is difficult to maintain full attention and interest for longer than 20 to 50 minutes.

Recall after learning

One of the least understood or appreciated aspects of memory and learning is what we recall immediately after learning.

This is what people think happens with their memory after studying or being lectured at for one hour. If you ask them to guess, they correctly think recall goes down fairly steeply in five days. However, the one thing they miss out changes everything.

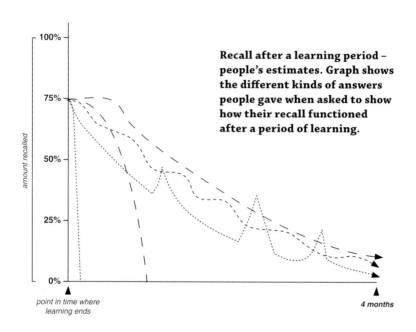

Recall after a learning period – people's estimates. Graph shows the different kinds of answers people gave when asked to show how their recall functioned after a period of learning.

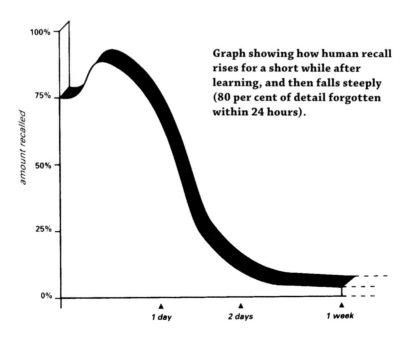

Graph showing how human recall rises for a short while after learning, and then falls steeply (80 per cent of detail forgotten within 24 hours).

The graph of recall after learning actually *rises* after learning, while the data is 'sinking in': your brain needs time to integrate, to Mind Map. Your brain needs integration and association of the last stuff just learned with the first stuff you learned in that session – and that's what happens in that curve – if you don't review, your recall plummets 80 per cent in a day and the detail you've learned is lost. Your ability to remember not only goes down but busts through the bottom as you misremember what it is you learned, you get the facts in the wrong order, the chemical equation/vocabulary/mathematical formula incorrect, the history dates wrong, then you remember the wrong things and then you get angry because you're under pressure and you don't like exams, so you get into a monstrous negative spiral...

But if you had reviewed at that point, your short-term memory would have picked up and linked up and recalled after learning was self generated by simple five-minute reviews. It seems impossible, but it's true.

The value of repetition

New information is stored first in your short-term memory. To transfer information to your long-term memory takes rehearsal and practice. On average, you will need to repeat an action at least five times before the information is transferred permanently to your long-term memory; this means revisiting what you have learned, using one or more of the memory techniques on a regular basis. My recommendations are to review and repeat what you have learned:

- Shortly after you have learned it.
- One day after you have learned it.
- One week after you first learned it.

- One month after you first learned it.
- Three to six months after you first learned it.

With each period of recall, you are not only revisiting the information that you have learned; you will also be adding to your knowledge. Your creative imagination has a part to play in long-term memory, and the more you go over information you have learned, the more you will link it to other information and knowledge that you already retain. Refer back to the graph on page 57 to see an illustration of all this.

> **The more we learn, the more we remember.**
> **The more we remember, the more we learn.**

Take a break or carry on?

Imagine that you have decided to study for two hours and that the first half-an-hour has been pretty difficult, although you have been making some progress. At this point in time you find that understanding begins to improve and that your progress seems to be getting better and faster. Would you pat yourself on the back and take a break? Or would you decide to keep the new and better rhythm going by studying on for a while until you began to lose the fresh impetus?

Some 90 per cent of people asked those questions would carry on. Of those who would take a break, only a few would recommend the same thing to anyone else! And yet surprisingly the best answer *is* to take a break. The reason is that understanding may be continuously high, but the recall of that

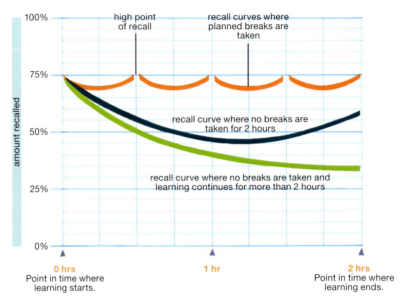

understanding will be getting worse if your mind is not given a break. It is essential that any time period for studying be broken down into 20–50 minute sections with small rests in between.

The graph above shows three different patterns of recall over a two-hour period of learning.

⊙ The top line includes four short breaks. The raised peaks show the moments when recall is highest. There are more high points on this line than in any of the other memory curves because there are four 'beginnings and endings'. Recall remains high.

⊙ The middle line shows a recall curve when no break is taken. The beginning and end points show the highest level of recall, but overall the retention drops to well below 75 per cent.

⊙ The bottom line shows what happens if no break is taken for a period of over two hours. This approach is obviously counter-productive as the recall line falls steadily downwards, to below the 50 per cent mark.

⊙ So the more well-spaced and short breaks we have, the more beginnings and endings we have, and the better our brain will be able to remember.

⊙ Brief breaks are also essential for relaxation: they relieve the muscular and mental tension that inevitably builds up during periods of intense concentration.

The common student practice of swotting five hours at a stretch for examination purposes should become a thing of the past, for understanding is not the same as remembering, as all too many failed examination papers bear witness.

The breaks themselves are also important for a number of reasons:

1 They give the body a physical rest and a chance to relax. This is always useful in a learning situation, and releases the build-up of tension.

2 They enable recall and understanding to 'work together' to the best advantage.

3 They allow a brief period of time for the just-studied information completely to relate each part of itself to the other part – to *intra-integrate*.

During each break the amount of knowledge that can immediately be recalled from the section just studied will increase and will be at a peak as the next section is commenced. This means that not only will more be recalled because the time period itself is best, but also that even more will be recalled because of the rest period.

To assist this even further, do a quick review of what you have read and a preview of what you are about to read at the beginning and end of each study period.

It has taken a number of pages to explain the necessity of deciding the best period of time for study and on an amount to be covered, but remember that the decisions themselves are extremely brief and will usually become automatic as you near completion of your browse. When these decisions have been made, the next step can be taken.

The core memory principles

Imagination and **Association** are at the heart of all the memory techniques in this chapter – they are also the foundation stones upon which BOST and Mind Maps are based. The more effectively you can use them, through key memory devices such as words, numbers and images, the more supercharged and effective your mind and memory will be.

Imagination

The more you stimulate and use your Imagination, the more you will enhance your ability to learn. This is because your Imagination has no limits; it is boundless and it stimulates your senses, and therefore your brain. Having an unlimited Imagination makes you more open to new experiences and less inclined to hold yourself back from learning new things.

Association

The most effective way to remember something is to think about it as an image, in Association with something else that is already fixed and known to you. If you ground your images in reality by associating them with something that is familiar, it will anchor them in a location, and you will be able to remember the information more easily. Association works by linking or pegging information to other information, such as the use of numbers, symbols, order and patterns.

As already explained, for your brain to work effectively you need to use both sides. It can be no coincidence that the two foundation-stones of memory are two main activities of your brain:

Imagination }
Association }   together they = **M**EMORY

Your memory gives you your sense of who you are, and so it is appropriate that the mnemonic to remember this is:

I AM

Imagination and Association are supported by the Ten Core Memory Principles. These principles help to anchor events in your memory and make it easier to recall them on demand.

Ten Core Memory Principles

To superpower your memory and help it to recall information efficiently, you will need to use every aspect of your mind. The Ten Core Memory Principles are designed to reinforce the strength of the impact of Imagination and Association on memory, and to trigger the involvement of as much of your extraordinary brainpower as possible. They are:

1 **Your senses**   6 **Symbols**
2 **Exaggeration**   7 **Order and patterns**
3 **Rhythm and movement**   8 **Attraction**
4 **Colour**   9 **Laughter**
5 **Numbers**   10 **Positive thinking**

The difference in impact is rather like using a 15-million-candlepower spotlight instead of your standard 4.5-volt-battery torch to illuminate your way home. You would experience the world more brightly and more brilliantly than ever before.

1   Senses

The more you can visualize, hear, taste, smell, feel or sense the thing that you are trying to recall, the better you will reinforce your ability to remember and be able to call to mind the information when you need it.

Everything you experience, everything you learn and everything you enjoy, is delivered to your brain via your senses:

Vision   Hearing   Smell
Taste   Touch
**Spatial awareness – of your body and
its movement**

The more sensitive you become to the information that your senses receive, the better you will be able to remember.

2   Exaggeration

Think large and be absurd in your imaginings. The more exaggerated your images are, in size, shape and sound, the better you will be able to remember them. Think of children's favourite characters: the cartoon ogre, Shrek, and the Harry Potter giant, Hagrid, are larger than life and stay alive in the mind's eye more readily than other characters in the films.

3   Rhythm and movement

Movement adds to the potential for something to be memorable to your brain.

- ⊙ Make your images move.
- ⊙ Make them three-dimensional.
- ⊙ Give them rhythm.

Movement helps your brain to 'link in' to the story and will help the sequence of data to become more extraordinary, and therefore memorable.

4   Colour

Colour brings memories alive and makes events more memorable. Whenever possible, use colour in your imaginings and in your drawings and notes so that your visual sense is heightened and your brain is stimulated to enjoy the experience of seeing.

5   Numbers

Numbers have a powerful impact on your memory because they bring order to your thoughts. Numbers help to make memories more specific.

6   Symbols

Symbols are a compact and coded way of using Imagination and Exaggeration to anchor memory. Creating a symbol to prompt a memory is rather like creating a logo. It tells a story and connects to, and is representative of, something larger than the image itself.

7   Order and patterns

Ordering your thoughts or putting them in sequence can be very useful when employed in conjunction with other memory principles. You might think about grouping thoughts by colour, weight or size, or order items by height, age or location.

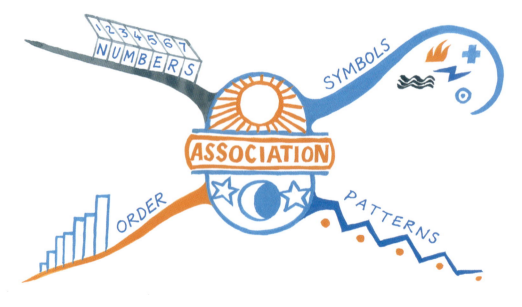

8 Attraction

We know what we like to look at and how we feel when we are attracted to someone or something. Your mind will remember an attractive image more readily than an unattractive one. Use your imagination to include attractive, positive images and associations as part of your memory.

9 Laughter

The more we laugh, the more we enjoy thinking about what we want to remember, and the easier it is to summon up information. Use humour, absurdity and a sense of fun to enhance your ability to remember and recall.

10 Positive thinking

In most instances, it is easier and more pleasant to recall positive images and experiences than negative ones. This is because your brain wants to return to things that make you feel

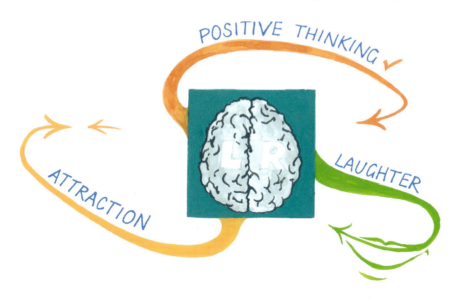

good about life and positive about your experiences. Negative associations and experiences are more likely to be blocked or modified by your brain. Think positive, and your Imagination and Associations will have more positive power.

Note: Key Words and Key Images

As you will find out in Chapters 6 and 7, it is easier to recall and Mind Map using Key Images and Key Words. One will trigger the other in your memory and these triggers are the pegs on which you will learn to hang all the other items you want to remember. They apply to the following two key memory systems which are essential aids to your studying success.

Two key memory systems to aid your studies

1 The Number–Shape System

⊙ This is ideal for short-term memory use, for recalling those items that you need to remember for only a few hours.

⊙ Each of the numbers is anchored to a constant set of images that you choose yourself.

The Number–Shape System is simple. All you have to do is think of an image for each of the numbers from one to ten. Follow the example below but, as we are all different, the images that will work best for you are ones that you choose and create for yourself. Once you understand the system, modify the words and images to fit your own imagination.

Each Key Image acts as a visual reminder of the number with which it is associated. Images should be strong and simple: easy to draw, easy to visualize and remember. The following list of associations shows classic examples:

1	paintbrush	6	elephant's trunk
2	swan	7	cliff
3	heart	8	snowman
4	yacht	9	balloon on stick
5	hook	10	bat and ball

After practising, you will automatically see in your mind's eye the image of a yacht, for example, when you think of the number four; or a swan when you think of the number two.

Each of us is different and the numbers will conjure up different images for different people. Give yourself about ten minutes to think of any other alternatives that you may prefer to those listed above and choose the one image for each number that works best for you. These will become your Key Number–Shape Memory images.

Use the space provided on the next page to write each number and draw the images that you have chosen to represent each digit.

⊙ Don't worry about how 'good' or 'bad' your images are.
⊙ Do use colour to bring the images alive and to reinforce them in your memory.
⊙ Do use also exaggeration, and movement.

1 When you have completed the task, close your eyes and run through the numbers from one to ten to ensure that you have remembered each of the image associations.

2 Then count backwards from ten to one, doing the same thing.

3 Practise recalling numbers at random until the Number–Shape image association becomes second-nature.

4 The idea is that the image, rather than the number, will gradually become synonymous with the numerical order.

5 Once you are comfortable that you can instantly recall the Number–Shape images, you can begin to use them in a study scenario. Simply peg the Number–Shape images to other words and then link them together by creating imaginative associations.

The Number–Shape System in action

Take a look at the following list of items:

1 symphony
2 prayer
3 watermelon
4 volcano
5 motorcycle
6 sunshine
7 apple pie
8 blossoms
9 spaceship
10 field of wheat

⊙ In your mind's eye, think of the Number–Shape images on page 124 that you have chosen to represent the numbers one to ten.

◉ Peg those Key Images to each of the words in the list above.
◉ Then create an imaginative image to link each of the pegged pairings.
◉ Create associations that are outrageous, crazy and colourful, so that you are better able to remember them.

For example, when paired with the words on the list, my Number–Shape memory keys are:

1	**paintbrush**	+ symphony
2	**swan**	+ prayer
3	**heart**	+ watermelon
4	**yacht**	+ volcano
5	**hook**	+ motorcycle
6	**elephant's trunk**	+ sunshine
7	**cliff**	+ apple pie
8	**snowman**	+ blossoms
9	**balloon and stick**	+ spaceship
10	**bat and ball**	+ field of wheat

The links could be as follows:
1   For symphony you might imagine a conductor, conducting frantically, with a gigantic paintbrush.
2   Prayer is an abstract word, which can be represented by adding form to the image. Try imagining your swan with its wings upheld like hands in prayer.
3   With a little imagination your watermelon can be transformed into a heart-shaped fruit, beating.
4   Imagine a gigantic volcano within the ocean that erupts red and furious beneath your yacht.
5   Imagine a heavy hook coming down from the sky and

lifting you and your speeding motorcycle off the road.

6 Imagine rays of sunshine pouring out of an elephant's trunk.

7 Your cliff could be made entirely of apple pie.

8 Imagine a snowman in springtime covered from head to foot in sweet blossoms.

9 Imagine a miniature spaceship that has flown into your balloon and stick and caused it to burst.

10 Imagine the shock as your bat cracks against the ball, and the ball is sent flying across a golden and windswept field of wheat.

You get the idea.

It is when you start to create your own sequences that you will feel this technique working. Don't just read the examples given here; create your own. The more absurd, over-the-top and sensual you are able to make your associations, the better you will tap into your own imagination. The more you practise, the easier the technique will be, and eventually, it will become second-nature.

2 The Number–Rhyme System

Easy to learn and based on a similar principle to the Number–Shape System, this is ideal for use when you need to remember short lists of items for a brief period of time.

The Number–Rhyme System differs from the Number–Shape System only in that it uses rhyming sounds rather than associated shapes as memory triggers for the numbers one to ten. The words you choose should conjure up strong but simple images, be easy to draw and easy to visualize and remember.

The following list of rhyming words will start you off:

1 **bun**
2 **shoe**
3 **tree**
4 **door**
5 **hive**
6 **sticks**
7 **heaven**
8 **skate**
9 **vine**
10 **hen**

Use your imagination – if you wish different images – to come up with alternative, memorable rhymes that work for you.

Choose words that are easy for you to remember and associate with each number, and draw your images in the boxes on the next page – using as much colour and imagination as possible.

⊙ To help create the clearest mental picture possible for each image, close your eyes and imagine projecting the image onto the inside of your eyelid – or onto a screen inside your head.

⊙ Hear, feel, smell and experience the image that works best for you.

When you have completed the task, close your eyes and run through the numbers from one to ten to ensure that you have remembered each of the rhyming image associations. Then count backwards from ten to one, doing the same thing.

The more you practise these techniques, the more your associative and creative thinking abilities will improve.

⊙ Practise recalling numbers at random until the Number–Rhymes and image association becomes second-nature.

The Number–Rhyme System in action

Once you have memorized your Number–Rhyme Key Words and Images you will be ready to put the Number–Rhyme System into action. Start by using the list of items below:

1 table
2 feather
3 cat
4 leaf
5 student
6 orange
7 car
8 pencil
9 shirt
10 poker

Refer back and you will see that the Number–Rhyme pairings would become:

1 **bun**   + table
2 **shoe**   + feather
3 **tree**   + cat
4 **door**   + leaf
5 **hive**   + student
6 **sticks**   + orange
7 **heaven**   + car
8 **skate**   + pencil
9 **vine**   + shirt
10 **hen**   + poker

The Key Memory Words are in bold. These are your memory triggers and remain consistent, no matter what else you are trying to remember.

Use Imagination and Association to create links between the pairs of words, perhaps as follows:

1   Imagine a giant **bun** on top of a fragile table which is in the process of crumbling from the weight. Smell the fresh cooked aroma; taste your favourite bun.

2   Imagine your favourite **shoe** with an enormous feather growing out of the inside, preventing you from putting your shoe on, tickling your foot.

3   Imagine a large **tree** with either your own cat or a cat you know, stuck in the very top branches, frantically scrambling about and mewing loudly.

4   Imagine your bedroom **door** is a giant leaf, crunching and rustling as you open it.

5   Imagine a student at his desk, dressed in black and yellow stripes, buzzing busily in a **hive** of activity, or with honey dripping on his pages.

6   Imagine large **sticks** puncturing the juicy surface of an orange that is as big as a beach ball. Feel and smell the juice of the orange squirting out.

7   Imagine the angels in **heaven** sitting on cars rather than clouds; experience yourself driving the car you think is heavenly.

8   Imagine yourself **skating** over the pavement, hearing the sound of the wheels on the ground, as you see the multi-coloured pencils attached to your skates creating fantastic coloured shapes wherever you go.

9   Imagine a **vine** as large as Jack and the Beanstalk's bean stalk, and instead of leaves on the vine, picture brightly coloured shirts hanging all over it, blowing in the wind.

10 Now it's your turn... Imagine a **hen**, with a poker...

Check that all the word and image associations are strong, positive, simple and clear, and make sure they are working for you. You can be sure that each time you practise, your technique will improve rapidly, and your memory will perform well above average.

> **Both key memory systems will give a supercharge boost to your recall and remembering powers – vital tools in cracking those revision barriers to exams, diplomas, coursework and other studies. Indeed, these two concepts lead straight to the development of Mind Maps. Mind Maps are an associated network of images which incorporate all the main elements of memory theory and left and right brain information.**

Here is a memory Mind Map. Mind Maps boost your memory by drawing on Key Words and Key Images. You will discover the power of Mind Maps in Chapter 6.

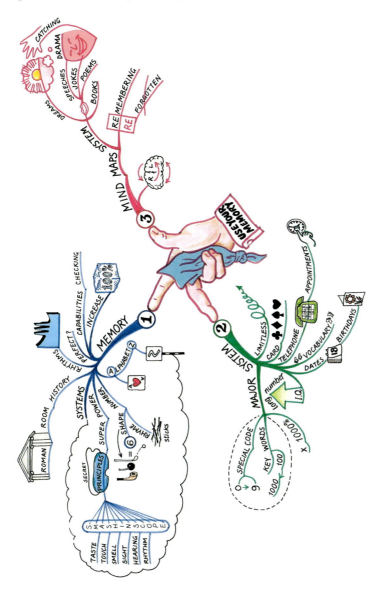

Onword

Now that you have discovered all the main elements of learning, and have seen how Speed Reading and Memory can be applied to your BOST technique, in the final chapters I will take you step by step through Mind Mapping to a totally comprehensive and easy-to-manage study programme.

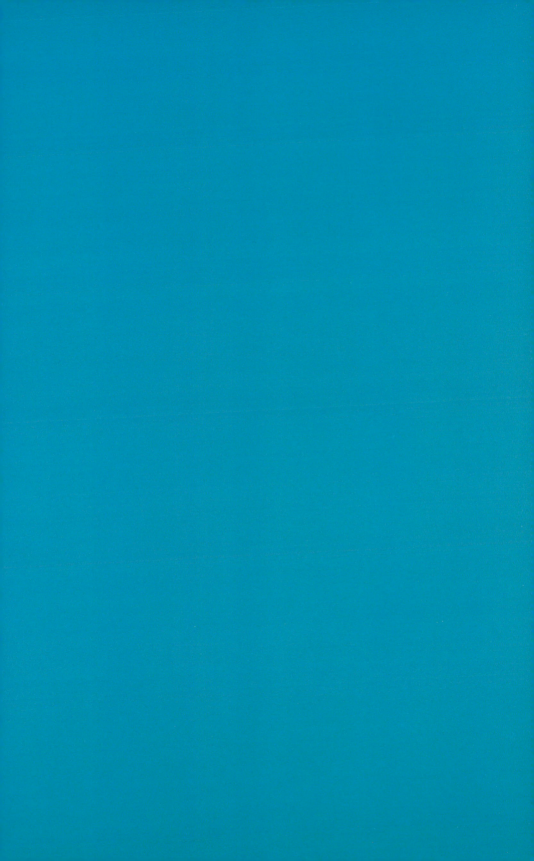

6 MIND MAPS®

Welcome to Mind Mapping – the core study skill for note-taking and note-making, preparing for essays and examinations, and the ground-breaking tool for transforming research and revision planning into smarter and faster activities.

The creation of a Mind Map® is a revolutionary way to tap into the infinite resources in your brain. I first developed it as a learning and memory method whilst struggling to take effective notes in my student days. So it couldn't be more relevant as a study skill. It is not merely a visual *aide memoire*; it is also a dynamic and organic revision tool, time manager and memory stimulator.

What is a Mind Map®?

Mind Maps are a graphic, networked method of storing, organizing and prioritizing information (usually on paper) using key or trigger words and images, each of which will 'snap on' specific memories and encourage new thoughts and ideas. Each of the memory triggers in a Mind Map is a key to unlocking facts, ideas and information and, also, to releasing the true potential of your amazing mind.

The clue to the Mind Map's effectiveness lies in its dynamic shape and form. It is drawn in the shape and form of a brain cell and is designed to encourage your brain to work in a way that is fast, efficient, and in the style that it does naturally.

Every time we look at the veins of a leaf or the branches of a tree we see nature's 'Mind Maps' echoing the shapes of brain cells and reflecting the way we ourselves are created and connected. Like us, the natural world is forever changing and regenerating, and has a communication structure that appears similar to our own. A Mind Map is a natural thinking tool that draws upon the inspiration and effectiveness of these natural structures.

Mind Maps are particularly adaptive for reading, revising, note-taking and planning for exams efficiently. They are invaluable for gathering and ordering information, and for identifying the key trigger words and facts from:

⊙ Reference, books, textbooks, primary and secondary source books.

⊙ Lectures, tutorials, course notes, research material.

⊙ Your own head.

They help you to manage information effectively, and increase the potential for personal success. Those students who use Mind Maps usually report that they feel a sense of confidence, that their aims are achievable, and that they are on track for reaching their goals.

Linear *v.* whole brain thinking

Because we speak and write in sentences, we have assumed that ideas and information should be stored in a linear, or list-like, fashion. This is self-limiting, as we shall see.

In speech we are limited to saying only one word at a time; likewise, in print, words are presented in lines and sentences, with a beginning, middle and end. This linear emphasis continues in schools, colleges and universities, where students are encouraged to take notes in sentence and bullet-point form.

The limitation of this approach is that it can take quite a while to get to the core issue of the matter, and during this process you will say, hear or read a great deal that is not essential for long-term recall.

We now know the brain is multi-dimensional, perfectly capable of, and *designed for*, taking in information that is non-linear, and that it does so all the time: when looking at photographs, pictures or interpreting the images and environment that are around you every day. Your brain, when listening to a series of spoken sentences, does not absorb information word by word, line by line; it takes in the information as a whole, sorts it, interprets it, and feeds it back to you in a multitude of ways. Whole-brain thinking is exactly the premise of the BOST® programme – see Chapters 3 and 7. You hear each word and put it in the context of existing knowledge as well as the other words around it. You do not need to have heard the entire range of sentences before forming a response. Key Words are critical 'signposts' or 'joggers' to your multi-dimensional data sorter, your brain.

Key Words and Key Images

The word 'Key' in front of the words 'Word' or 'Image' means much more than 'this is important'. It means this is a 'Memory Key'. The Key Word or Key Image is being developed as a critically important trigger to stimulate your mind, and unlock and retrieve your memories.

A **Key Word** is a special word that has been chosen or created to become a unique reference point for something important that you wish to remember. Words stimulate the left side of your brain and are a vital component of mastering memory; but they are not as powerful on their own as when you take the time to draw them and transform them into a

Key Image. An effective Key Image will stimulate both sides of your brain and draw upon all your senses. Key Images are at the very heart of my Mind Mapping and BOST programme.

Here is a simple example of how a Key Word and Key Image can boost your memory:

⊙ When trying to find an image to encapsulate the concept of environmental water and waste management and the problems of water shortage, you might choose the word 'tap'.

⊙ The word 'tap' will, as a Key Word, trigger your analytical left-brain memory.

⊙ Drawing a picture of a tap, with perhaps a drop of water dripping out, will create a Key Image, which will engage your visual right-brain memory.

⊙ The picture will become a visual trigger that will represent not only the written word, but also water and waste management as an industry with its attendant hosepipe bans, leaking pipes and declining reservoir reserves.

The word on its own is not enough to trigger recall of all your studies of water energy, because it is not engaging your whole brain. The word as part of a sentence will not trigger the entire experience either, because a sentence defines and limits. The purpose of a Key Word that has been transformed into a drawn Key Image, on the other hand, is to connect with both the left-brain and the right-brain functions. This action will radiate connections and trigger recall of complete associated information.

Here's another example of how your brain can lock into a Key Word:

⊙ You telephone a talking timetable to receive information about the 18.50 train from your college digs to your family home.

Before the automatic voice has made any mention of your home town, you are told that there are delays that evening at a city along the line, the first stop just outside station from your college.

⊙ In a split second, your brain will begin to make associations: feelings associated with returning home, or sleeping in a comfortable bed; the sounds of people's voices and platform announcements; the smell and taste of a delicious evening meal. All of which leave you weighing up whether to make the journey by coach, or stay overnight and get the morning train.

⊙ The reason for this response is that the word 'delay' has acted as a Key Word that has triggered a multi-faceted response before you have heard one word of specific information relating to your original question, and before the talking timetable has finished its sentence.

⊙ Getting home is still your main aim – but the delay has, for the present time, become the central concept.

So Key Words and their context are vitally important memory joggers, and it is the network inside your mind that is of most importance in helping to understand and interpret them.

Key Words – cut the verbiage

We are so used to speaking and writing words that we have come to believe that normal sentences are the best way to store and recall verbal images and ideas. In fact, over 90 per cent of written notes taken by students are superfluous, because your brain naturally prefers Key Words that represent the big picture. This means that:

> O Time is wasted recording words that have no bearing on memory.
>
> O Time is wasted re-reading unnecessary words.
>
> O Time is wasted searching for Key Words that have not been highlighted in any way and therefore blend in with the whole.
>
> O Time is wasted when the connections between Key Words are slowed down by extraneous connecting words.
>
> O Distance weakens associations between Key Words. The further apart they are, the weaker the associations.

The language of your brain

Key Words are crucial and so are Key Images. Remember, the main language of your brain is neither the spoken nor the written word. Your brain works via your senses by creating associations between images, colours, Key Words and ideas. Put in a nutshell: Imagination and Association. These are connected to whole-brain activity and both are stimulated mainly when you use:

- Your senses.
- Exaggeration.
- Rhythm and movement.
- Colour.
- Laughter.
- Pictures and images.

- Numbers.
- Words.
- Symbols.
- Order.
- Patterns.

We are all attracted to people who make us feel good, and things that we enjoy. In order for your Mind Map to become something that you enjoy looking at, and want to keep referring to, it needs to be:

- A positive representation of events or plans.
- Attractive to look at.

A Mind Map that includes these important factors will encourage your brain to associate, link and connect your thoughts, fears, dreams and ideals in ways that are far more creative than any other form of note-taking. A Mind Map triggers associations in your brain that will help you to link key revision ideas more quickly and creatively than any other form of 'brainstorming'.

Mind Maps are better than standard note-taking.
A Mind Map has a number of advantages over standard note-taking:
- The central idea is more clearly defined.
- The relative importance of each idea is clearly identified.
- The more important ideas are immediately

recognizable at the centre of the Mind Map.

O The links between key concepts are immediately identifiable – via Key Words – encouraging association of ideas and concepts and improving memory.

O Review of information is effective and rapid.

O The structure of a Mind Map allows additional concepts to be added easily.

O Each Mind Map is a unique creation – which will in turn aid accurate recall.

Radiant Thinking® for optimum revision

To understand why Mind Maps are so effective, it is helpful to know more about the way your brain thinks and remembers information. As explained above, your brain does not think in a linear, monotonous way. Rather it thinks in multiple directions simultaneously, starting from central trigger points in Key Images and Key Words, which are explained on page 140: what I call Radiant Thinking®. As the term suggests, thoughts radiate outward like the branches of a tree, the veins of a leaf or the blood vessels of the body that emanate from the heart. In the same way, a Mind Map starts with the central concept and **radiates** outwards to take in the detail, mirroring effectively the activity of your brain.

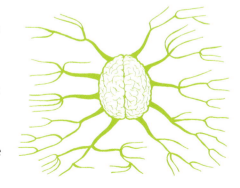

The more closely you can record information in a way that reflects the natural workings of your brain, the more efficiently your brain will be able to trigger the recall of essential facts and personal memories. To show you what I mean, try the following exercise.

Radiant Thinking® exercise 1

Most people believe that the brain thinks linguistically. I am going to ask you to access a piece of data from that vast database, your brain. You will have no time to think about it in advance. I would like you to consider the following questions, once you have accessed the piece of data:

- What was it that you accessed?
- How long did it take you to access it?
- Was there colour?
- What were the associations around the data?

Now, here is the data:

BANANA

Most people are familiar with what a banana looks like. When you 'heard' the word you may have seen the colours yellow, brown, or green – depending on the ripeness of the fruit. You may have seen its curved shape. You may have associated the image with a fruit salad, breakfast cereal or a milk shake. The image will have appeared instantaneously, as if from nowhere, and you are unlikely to have spent any time visualizing the letters of the word. The image was already stored in your mind; you simply needed to trigger its release. We learn from this that ultimately we think in images and not words.

This quick test shows that everyone, whatever their sex, status or nationality, uses Radiant Thinking to link Key Word associations with Key Images – instantaneously (see below). This is the basis for all our thinking and this is the basis of Mind Maps. **Mind Maps have been devised to enhance and increase your Radiant Thinking processes.**

Radiant Thinking® exercise 2

You are going to complete a mini Mind Map to represent the concept of 'happiness'. There is space around the word for ten Key Word associations.

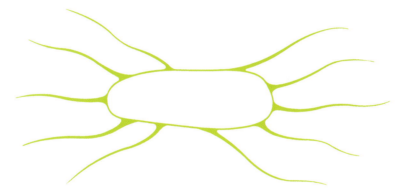

⊙ First draw a central image that represents 'happiness' for you.

⊙ Then, on each of the branches around the edge, write the first ten Key Word associations that radiate from the centre when you think of the picture you have drawn to represent 'happiness'.

⊙ It is important to put down the first words that come to mind, no matter how ridiculous you may think they are. Don't self-censor or give yourself pause for thought.

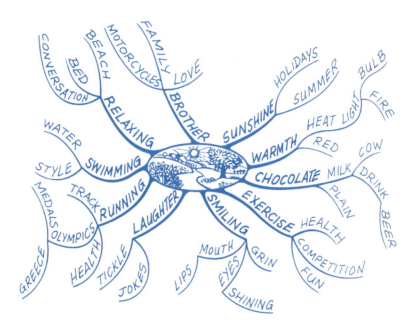

⊙ If you find it easy to think of more than ten words, include them by drawing extra branches for them.

⊙ When you have finished, compare your results with the example above to see which words overlap.

The point of this exercise is to show that once your brain begins to 'freewheel' in word association, it doesn't slow down. Rather like following links on the Internet, you will find yourself thinking of many more connections.

How to prepare a Mind Map®

A Mind Map represents a personal thought-journey on paper, and like any successful journey it needs some planning in order to be successful. The first step before starting your Mind Map is to decide where you are headed:

- What is your goal or vision?
- What are the sub-goals and categories that contribute to your goal?
- Are you planning a study project?
- Are you brainstorming ideas to prepare an essay?
- Do you need to note-take an upcoming lecture?
- Are you preparing a plan for an entire term's coursework?

Making this decision is important because a successful Mind Map has at its heart a core image which represents your goal, and your first step will be to draw a picture in the centre of your Mind Map to represent that goal as a success.

Think pictorially and think in colour

The adage that 'a picture is worth a thousand words' is true. In an experiment, scientists showed a group of people 600 images at a rate of one per second. When tested for accurate recall after the presentation, there was a 98 per cent rate of accurate recall across the whole group. The human brain finds it much easier to remember images than words and this is why, in a Mind Map, the central key idea is expressed as an image. Using images elsewhere in your Mind Map is also important. To practise your image-association skills, look back at Radiant Thinking exercise 2 for the word 'happiness'. See whether you can re-create the whole Mind Map using images only.

To make sure that your Mind Map becomes a genuinely useful tool that you want to develop, the central image needs to make you feel positive and focused when you look at it. Therefore think in colour, preferably multi-colours rather than boring monochrome. It does not need to be beautifully drawn or wonderfully artistic. Create a positive vision, and it will take on a life and energy of its own and will help you to stay focused. When you are focused you become the human equivalent of a very powerful laser beam: precise, goal-directed and phenomenally powerful.

Basic Ordering Ideas

You now need to add structure to the Mind Mapping of your ideas. The first step is to decide on your Basic Ordering Ideas (BOIs). BOIs are the 'hooks' on which to hang all associated ideas (just as the chapter headings of a textbook represent the thematic content within the pages). BOIs are the chapter headings of your thoughts: the words or images that represent the simplest and most obvious categories of information. They are the words that will automatically attract your brain to think of the greatest number of associations.

If you are not sure what your BOIs should be, ask yourself the following simple questions with regard to your main goal or vision:

- What knowledge is required to achieve my aim?
- If this were a book, what would the chapter headings be?
- What are my specific objectives?
- What are the seven most important categories in this subject area?
- What are the answers to my seven basic questions: Why? What? Where? Who? How? Which? When?
- Is there a larger, more encompassing category that all of these fit into that would be more appropriate to use?

For example, a Mind Map of life plans might include the following useful personal BOI categories:

Personal history: past, present, future
Strengths   **Weaknesses**   **Likes**   **Dislikes**
Long-term goals   **Family**   **Friends**
Achievements   **Hobbies**   **Emotions**
Work   **Home**   **Responsibilities**

The advantages of having well-thought-out BOIs are:

⊙ The primary ideas are in place, so the secondary ideas will follow and flow more naturally.

⊙ The BOIs help to shape, sculpt and construct the Mind Map, so encouraging your mind to think in a naturally structured way.

When you decide upon your first set of BOIs before you begin Mind Mapping, the rest of your ideas will flow in a far more coherent and useful way.

Pen to paper

To create effective Mind Maps you will need:

⊙ A stock of paper: make sure you have a blank exercise book filled with plain pages, or a quantity of good-quality, large-sized sheets of blank, unlined paper.

⊙ A range of multi-coloured pens in fine, medium and highlighter thickness.

⊙ At least 10–20 minutes of uninterrupted time.

⊙ Your brain.

More on paper

⊙ You need plenty of paper, because this is not just a practical exercise – it is a personal journey. You will want to refer back to your Mind Maps over time to assess your progress and to review your goals.

⊙ You need large-sized sheets of paper because you will want space to explore your ideas. Small pages will cramp your style.

⊙ The pages should be blank and unlined in order to free your brain to think in a non-linear, uninhibited and creative way.

⊙ An exercise book or ring binder of paper is best because your first Mind Map is the start of a working journal. You don't want to be subconsciously inhibited by a need to be 'neat', and you will want to keep all your ideas together in order to see how your plans and needs evolve over time.

More on pens

⊙ You need easy-flowing pens because you will want to be able to read what you have created and may want to write fast.

⊙ A selection of colours is important because colour stimulates your brain and will activate creativity and visual memory.

⊙ Colour also allows you to introduce structure, weight and emphasis to your Mind Map.

Mind Map® skills in detail

1   Use emphasis

Always use a central image

⊙ An image automatically focuses your eye and your brain. It triggers numerous associations and is a highly effective memory aid.

⊙ In addition, an image that is appealing will please you and draw attention to itself.

⊙ If a word, rather than a picture, is used as the central image, it can be made more three-dimensional by the addition of shade, colour or attractive lettering.

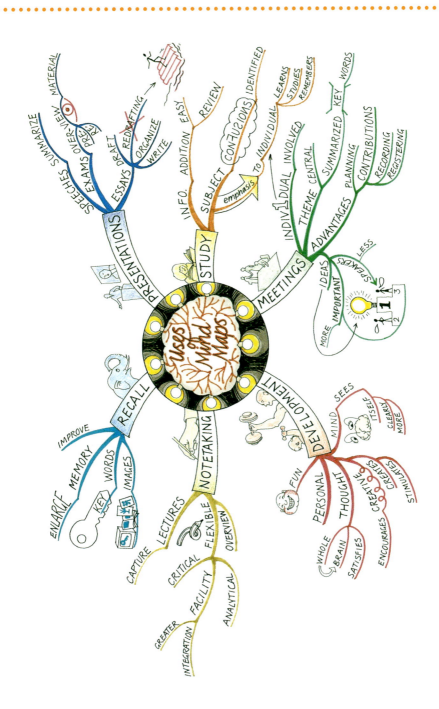

Uses of Mind Maps

Use images throughout your Mind Map®

⊙ Using images throughout your Mind Map will add more focus and make it more attractive. It will also help you to 'open your mind' to the world around you, and will stimulate both the left brain and the right brain in the process.

⊙ Use three or more colours per central image. Colours stimulate memory and creativity: they wake up your brain. This is in contrast to monochrome (one-colour) images, which your brain sees as monotonous, and which send it to sleep.

⊙ Use dimension both in images and around words. This will help things to stand out, and whatever stands out is more easily remembered. Using dimension is especially effective in giving Key Words prominence.

Use variations of printing, line and image

⊙ Varying the size of the type will introduce a sense of hierarchy and give a clear message regarding the relative importance of the items listed.

Use organized spacing

⊙ Organizing the look of the branches on the page will help communicate the hierarchy and categorization of ideas, and will also make it easier to read and more attractive to look at. Leave the right amount of space around each item on your Mind Map, partly so that each item can be seen clearly, and partly because space itself is an important part of communicating a message.

2 Use association

Use arrows

⊙ Use arrows when you want to make connections within and across the branches.

⊙ Arrows guide your eye in a way that will automatically join things together. Arrows also suggest movement. Movement is a valuable aid to effective memory and recall.

⊙ Arrows can point in one direction, or in several directions at once, and they can be of all shapes and sizes.

Use colours

⊙ Colour is one of the most powerful tools for enhancing memory and creativity.

⊙ Choosing specific colours for coding purposes will give you faster access to the information contained in your Mind Map and will help you to remember it more easily.

⊙ Colour-coding is especially useful for group Mind Mapping.

Use codes

⊙ Codes save you a lot of time. They enable you to make instant connections between different parts of your Mind Map, however far apart they may be on the page.

⊙ Codes may take the form of ticks, crosses, circles, triangles or underlining, or they can be more elaborate.

3   Be clear

Use only one Key Word per line

⊙ Each individual word will conjure up many thousands of its own possible connotations and associations.

⊙ By placing one word per line, you have maximum opportunity to make associations for each word. In addition every word is connected to the word or image that sits alongside it on the next line. In this way, your brain is opened up to new thoughts.

⊙ Using one Key Word per line gives that Key Word, and therefore your mind, freedom to radiate out in all possible directions. This rule is the opposite of a restriction. If you can use it well, it sets your mind free to explore its infinite creative potential.

Print all words

⊙ Printed words are more defined in shape and are therefore easier for your mind to 'photograph' and retain.

⊙ The extra time it takes to print a word is more than made up for by the advantages it creates of increased speed of association and recall.

⊙ Printing also encourages brevity, and can be used to emphasize the relative importance of words.

Print Key Words on lines

⊙ The lines on a Mind Map are important as they connect the individual Key Words together.

⊙ Your Key Words need to be connected to the lines to help your brain make the connection with the rest of your Mind Map.

Make line length equal to word length

⊙ If words and their lines are of equal length they will look more effective and will connect more easily to the words on either side of them.

⊙ The space saved will allow you to add more information to your Mind Map.

Connect lines to other lines and major branches to the central image

⊙ Connecting the lines on your Mind Map will help you to connect the thoughts in your mind.

⊙ Lines can be transformed into arrows, curves, loops, circles, ovals, triangles or any other shape you choose.

Make the central lines thicker and keep them curved

⊙ Thicker lines will send the message to your brain that they are the most important, so thicken up all central lines. If, to begin with, you are uncertain which ideas are going to be the most important, you can thicken the lines once you have finished.

Create shapes and boundaries around your Mind Map® branches

⊙ Shapes encourage your imagination.

⊙ Creating shapes in your Mind Map – for example, by creating a shape around a branch of a Mind Map – will help you to remember the many themes and ideas more easily.

Make your images as clear as possible

⊙ Clarity on the page encourages clarity of thought. A clear Mind Map will also be more elegant, graceful and pleasant to use.

Keep the paper arranged horizontally in front of you

⊙ The 'landscape' format of the page will give you optimum freedom to draw and create your Mind Map.

⊙ It will also be easier to read once you have finished it.

Keep printing as upright as possible

⊙ Upright printing gives your brain easier access to the thoughts expressed on the page; this applies to the angle of the lines as well as of the words.

4   Use hierarchy

⊙ The way you lay out and structure your Mind Map will have an immense impact on how you use it, and its practical 'usability'.

5   Use numerical order

⊙ If your Mind Map is the basis for, say, a core topic, you will need to order your thoughts – whether chronologically or in order of importance.

⊙ To do this, simply number the branches in the desired order of action or priority.

⊙ Other levels of detail, such as dates, can be added if preferred. Letters of the alphabet could also be used, instead of numbers.

6   Develop a personal style

You will relate to, and remember more easily, something that you have created yourself.

What to avoid when Mind Mapping

There are three danger areas that face any Mind Mapper:

1   The creation of Mind Maps that aren't really Mind Maps.

2   Using phrases instead of single words.

3   Unnecessary concern about creating a 'messy' Mind Map, and a negative emotional response as a result.

1   When a Mind Map® is not a Mind Map®

Take a look at the following cluster shapes. Each of them represents an early Mind Map drawn by someone who hasn't quite grasped the basics.

At first glance they may seem acceptable, but in fact they ignore the key principle of Radiant Thinking. Each idea is on its own, cut off from the others. There is no dynamic connection

3 When a *messy* Mind Map® is a *good* Mind Map®

Depending on your circumstances when note-taking, you may not always be able to create a neat and tidy Mind Map. If you are in a lecture where ideas are not being presented in an ordered fashion, it will not always be possible to identify immediately the core concepts. Your Mind Map will reflect that organic situation and will be an accurate reflection of your state of mind at the time.

However 'messy' the Mind Map is, it is still likely to contain more information of value than would have been the case had you noted everything down. Take some time immediately after such a lecture to transform your Mind Map notes into a more constructive form. Use:

- Arrows.
- Symbols.
- Highlighting.
- Images.

and other devices, to identify the Basic Ordering Ideas and to instil hierarchy, associations and colour into your notes. If necessary, re-draw your Mind Map following the basic rules, so that the information is made easier for your memory to recall in future.

How to create a Mind Map®

1 **Focus** on the core question, the precise topic. Be clear about what it is that you are aiming for or trying to resolve.

2 Turn your first sheet of paper **sideways** in front of you (landscape-style), in order to start creating your Mind Map

in the centre of the page. This will allow you freedom of expression, without being restricted by the narrow measure of the page.

3 Draw an **image** in the centre of the blank sheet of paper to represent your goal. Don't worry if you feel that you can't draw well; that doesn't matter. It is very important to use an image as the starting point for your Mind Map because an image will jump-start your thinking by activating your imagination.

4 Use **colour** from the outset, for emphasis, structure, texture, creativity – to stimulate visual flow and reinforce the image in your mind. Try to use at least three colours overall, and create your own colour-coding system. Colour

can be used hierarchically or thematically, or it can be used to emphasize certain points.

5 Now draw a series of **thick lines**, radiating out from the centre of the image. These are the primary branches of your Mind Map and will support your idea like the sturdy branches of a tree.

Make sure you **connect** these primary branches firmly to the central image, because your brain, and therefore your memory, operates by association.

6   **Curve** your lines because they are more interesting to your eye and more memorable to your brain than straight ones.

7   Write one **Key Word** on each branch, that you associate with the topic. These are your **Main Thoughts** (and your Basic Ordering Ideas), relating to themes such as:

Situation   **Feelings**   **Facts**   **Choices**

Remember that using only one Key Word per line allows you to define the very essence of the issue you are exploring,

whilst also helping to make the association be stored more emphatically in your brain. Phrases and sentences limit the effect and confuse your memory.

8   Add a few **empty branches** to your Mind Map. Your brain will want to put something on them.

9   Next, create second- and third-level branches for your related **Associated** and **Secondary Thoughts**. The secondary level connects to the primary branches, the third level to the secondary branches, and so on. Association is everything in this process. The words that you choose for each of your branches might include themes that ask questions: the Who, What, Where, Why, How of the subject or situation.

Ideas into action

Your completed Mind Map is both a picture of your thoughts and the first stage in preparing a plan of action. Prioritizing and weighting your themes and conclusions can be done quite simply by numbering each branch of the Mind Map.

Make your most important study point 1, the next most important 2, then 3, 4 and so on.

Onword

Now that you have learned how to create a Mind Map, the next chapter examines the many exciting applications of your new-found skills to the crucial areas of your study using BOST.

7 REVOLUTIONIZE YOUR STUDY WITH MIND MAPS® AND BOST®

Now you are armed with all the information and skills you need in order to: study efficiently, organize effectively, read at least twice as fast, remember successfully what you have read and Mind Map so brilliantly that you will remember information 10 times better. Now you can incorporate the skills you have acquired into using BOST to Mind Map all your textbooks and study materials.

How to Mind Map® a textbook

Preparation

1 Browse – create the central image of the Mind Map (10 minutes).

2 Set time and amount targets (5 minutes).

3 Mind Map existing knowledge on the subject (10 minutes).

4 Define and Mind Map goals (5 minutes).

Application (times dependent on material studied)

5 Overview – add main Mind Map branches.

6 Preview – first and second levels.

7 Inview – fill in the Mind Map details.

8 Review – complete the Mind Map.

Preparation

1 Browse (10 minutes)

A **Speed reading**: Before you start reading the textbook in detail, it is essential to gain a quick overview. The best way is to look at the front and back cover and the list of contents, and, using a guide (a pencil or your finger), skim through the pages a few times, getting the general 'feel' of the book.

B **Mind Mapping**: Now take a large blank sheet, turn it sideways or landscape and draw a central image that summarizes the subject or title. If there is a particularly striking or colourful image on the cover or inside the book, feel free to use it.

C **Radiant Thinking**: If you are also reasonably sure of the main branches that are going to radiate from the centre, you can add these at the same time. They will often correspond to the major divisions or chapters of the book, or your specific objectives in reading it.

By starting your Mind Map at this early stage, you are giving your brain a central focus and the basic architecture within which it can integrate all the information gained from studying the book.

2 Setting time and amount targets (5 minutes)

In view of your study objectives, the book's content and level of difficulty, and the amount of knowledge you already have, decide on:

A The amount of time you will devote to the entire task.

B The amount you will cover in each study period.

3 Mind Mapping existing knowledge on the subject (10 minutes)

Now 'turn away' from the book and your previous Mind Map, take a new sheet of paper, and *as fast as you can* do a quick-fire Mind Map burst on everything you already know about the topic you are about to study. This will include whatever information you have gained from your initial browse through the book, plus any general knowledge or specific items of information you may have picked up during your whole life that relate to the topic in any way. Avoid simply jotting down headwords and data in linear form – you are practising Mind Mapping here.

Most students are delighted and surprised to find that they actually know a lot more about the topic than they had previously thought. This exercise is also especially valuable because it brings appropriate associations or 'grappling hooks' to the surface of your brain and sets it moving in the direction of the topic you are studying. It also enables you to identify areas of strength and weakness in your knowledge, indicating which aspects you need to supplement.

4   Defining and Mind Mapping goals (5 minutes)

At this stage you can either add to the existing knowledge Mind Map you have just completed, using a different-coloured pen, or you can take a new blank sheet and do another quick-fire Mind Map burst on your goals in reading the textbook or study guide. These goals may take the form of specific questions to which you wish to find the answers, or areas of knowledge about which you wish to find out more.

Mind Mapping your goals in this way greatly increases the probability of your eye/brain system registering any information it comes across that seems relevant to those goals. In effect, the Mind Map of your goals acts as an 'appetite' that naturally motivates your search. In the same way as a person who has not eaten for several days will become obsessed with food, good preparatory Mind Maps increase your 'hunger' for knowledge.

Application

5 – 8 Overview, Preview, Inview, Review (time dependent on study material)

Having completed your preparation, you are ready to start the four levels of reading – Overview, Preview, Inview and Review – which take you ever deeper into the content of the book. (This is where Speed Reading especially comes into its own – see Chapter 4.) You can now either Mind Map the book as you read, or mark the book while reading and complete your Mind Map afterwards.

⊙ Mind Mapping while you read is like having an ongoing 'conversation' with the author, reflecting the developing pattern of knowledge as the book progresses. The growing Mind Map also enables you to keep checking your level of understanding and adjusting the focus of your information gathering.

⊙ Mind Mapping afterwards means that you produce your Mind Map only once you have gained a complete understanding of the book's content, and the way each part relates to the others. Your Mind Map will therefore be more comprehensive and focused and less likely to require revision.

Whichever method you choose, it is important to remember that Mind Mapping a textbook or study guide is a two-way process. The aim is not simply to duplicate the author's thoughts in Mind Map form. Rather, it is a question of organizing and integrating his or her thoughts in the context of your own knowledge, understanding, interpretation and specific goals, for example, the likely exam questions. Your Mind Map should therefore ideally include your own comments, thoughts and creative realizations arising from what you have read. Using different colours or codes will enable you to distinguish your own contributions from those of the author.

To refresh your memory of the Application system generally see Chapter 3.

How to Mind Map® from lectures to DVDs

This is very similar to Mind Mapping a book, except that you are often subject to the linear progression of the lecture or visual presentation and do not have the luxury of being able to refer to different parts of the material at will, nor can you rely on speed reading to achieve fast learning.

For this reason, it is especially important to get an **Overview** of the topic as quickly as possible. Before the lecture, video, DVD or film begins, you should draw your central image and as many of the main branches as you can. (A good lecturer should be pleased to help anyone who shows an interest in their subject and give you a preview of the lecture showing the main areas he or she plans to cover.)

Again, before the lecture, video, DVD or film begins and if circumstances permit, you can do a quick-fire **two-minute Mind Map burst** of your existing knowledge on the subject, in order to prepare your brain to take in new information.

As time progresses, you can fill in the information and ideas on your original Mind Map wherever they seem most relevant, adjusting your basic structure if necessary. As with Mind Mapping a textbook, try to **clarify by colour coding** your own comments and contributions in response to those of the lecturer.

Case study of a Mind-Mapping student

Here's an example of a female student, Lana Israel, who used Mind Maps as a standard part of her study practice. Lana won a school Science competition using Mind Maps, and went on to win not only the State Science Fair Competition, but also the USA National Science Fair Competition. She was then contacted by Harvard University where she studied and achieved straight A grades and one surprising B grade. Not satisfied that her B grade was warranted, she presented her appeal case using Mind Maps, and was duly awarded the A grade she deserved. Her Mind Map is a combination of note-taking, and essay and exam preparation. As Lana said:

Mind Map by Lana Israel in preparation for a History exam.

'This Mind Map is taken straight from my history notes. My teacher usually lectures every day and naturally I Mind Map his lectures. This Mind Map deals with America's earliest political parties and their stands. The central image illustrates the split in politics which lead to the formation of two separate parties. Just by glancing at my image, I am made aware of the theme of the Map and general characteristics of the parties, Democrats being more common men and Federalists more concerned with aristocracy. The use of pictures in Mind Mapped notes is wonderful for chunking down concepts, recalling information and making history fun. The equivalent of this Map, linearly, is at least two to three pages of linear notes – studying three pages rather than one is certainly not fun. Furthermore, this Map can be reviewed in under a minute, saving time and enabling one to remember more as key words are strongly linked... Mind Maps have helped me get As in History – "A" Definite Advantage!'

Creating a Master Mind Map® for study

If you are involved in a long-term course of study it is a good idea to keep a giant Master Mind Map reflecting the major sub-divisions, themes, theories, personalities and events in that subject. Every time you read a textbook or go to a lecture, you can record any major new insight on your Master Mind Map, thus creating an external mirror image of your growing network of internal knowledge.

Those who have done this notice a surprising and rewarding trend. After a reasonable length of time, the boundaries of the Mind Map begin to edge into other subjects and disciplines. Thus the periphery of a Master Mind Map on psychology, for example, begins to touch on neurophysiology, mathematics, philosophy, astronomy, geography, meteorology, ecology, and so on.

This does not mean that your knowledge structure is disintegrating and moving too far from the point. It actually means that your knowledge is becoming so deep and extensive that it is beginning to relate to other areas of knowledge.

Mind Mapping for note-taking

The most effective speed-reading skills in the world need a note taking technique that supports them rather than, like linear-minded studying techniques, one that is time-consuming and ineffective. The Mind Map method of information storage and retrieval follows the same principles as speed reading, and it has been designed to work in synergy with your brain, which means that your knowledge levels will increase the more you use them.

A valid note-taking method must incorporate:

1   Planning, focus and preview.
2   Clear recognition, assimilation and comprehension of facts.
3   A reflection of existing levels of knowledge.
4   A way of retaining information.
5   Ease of recall.
6   An easy form of communicating the information.

A Mind Map fulfils all these criteria. Effective note-taking is not about slavishly reproducing everything that has been said; it is a selective process. It should minimize the number of words written down and maximize the amount of information recalled. Mind Maps help you achieve precisely that.

Disadvantages of 'normal' note-taking

⊙ A tendency to take indiscriminate notes without Preview, which means that the overall focus and intent are lost.

⊙ A preoccupation with 'getting everything down' on paper, which prevents ongoing critical analysis and appreciation of the subject matter.

⊙ Detailed note-taking bypasses the mind and distracts the listener who then misses what is really being said. (Just as it is possible to copy-type thousands of words of text without reading it.)

⊙ The volume of notes tends to become so great that the note-taker feels disinclined to refer back to them, or can make no sense of them, and has to begin again.

Key Words and Key Images revisited

The crucial element in effective note-taking is the selection of appropriate Key Words and Key Images that encapsulate the essence of everything you have read. These have already been described in Chapter 6, but to re-iterate at this crucial juncture:

The Key Words in your Mind Map:

1   Must trigger the right kind of memory.
2   Should not be too descriptive, abstract or general to be practical.
3   Must evoke a very specific image in your mind.
4   Must be personally satisfying.
5   Must have the ability to summarize information.

In Mind Map notes, instead of taking down whole sentences or making lists, a combination of Key Words and Key Images is used to capture the essence of the information and to act as precise memory triggers to recall the information.

As you build up your Mind Map, so your brain creates an integrated map of the whole of the territory you are recording. Your BOST Mind Map therefore becomes a multi-dimensional note from your own brain that reproduces all you want to remember in a unique fashion. It is a powerful graphic technique that harnesses the power of your brain to the full and unlocks your true potential. Mind Maps work with your memory, to make it easy for you to recall information on demand.

Reviewing your Mind Map® notes

Having completed your Mind Map notes, you should review them regularly in order to maintain your understanding and recall of what you have learnt. For a 1-hour period of study the optimum intervals and time limits for review after the study are as follows:

- After 10 minutes – take a 10-minute review.
- After 24 hours – take a 2–4-minute review.
- After a week – take a 2-minute review.
- After a month – take a 2-minute review.
- After six months – take a 2-minute review.
- After a year – take a 2-minute review.

The information will then be stored in your long-term memory. Rather than just looking at your original Mind Map for each review, it is best to start by doing another quick-fire Mind Map burst of what you remember. This will show what you are able to recall *without any assistance*. You can then check against your original Mind Map, adjusting any discrepancies and strengthening any areas of weak recall. Refer back to the graph on page 57 for a visual reminder of recall patterns .

Benefits of Mind Map® notes and the Master Mind Map®

1   They enable you to keep the whole knowledge 'picture' inview at all times, thus giving you a more balanced and comprehensive understanding of the subject in its entirety.
2   They take up far less space than linear notes. Between 10 and 1000 pages of text can be summarized on one large Mind Map page. **Use a Mind Map, save a tree!**
3   They give your brain a central focus and structure within which to integrate your knowledge of any subject.
4   They increase your brain's 'hunger' for knowledge.
5   They allow you to relate your own thoughts and ideas to those expressed in books, lectures or presentations.
6   They are far more effective and efficient for review purposes.
7   They enhance your memory and understanding of textbooks, study guides, lectures and coursework, enabling you to excel in any course of study.

Mind Mapping for essays

The Mind Maps we are discussing are meant to replace the voluminous linear notes that most students write before actually writing their essays.

Note-taking from a textbook or lecture involves taking the essential elements from linear material to generate a Mind Map (as described above).

Note-making for an essay means first identifying the essential elements of the subject in a Mind Map and then using your Mind Map notes to build a linear structure.

◉ As always, you should begin your Mind Map with a central image representing the subject of your essay.

◉ You can then select appropriate Basic Ordering Ideas (BOIs), as your major branches or principal sub-divisions. At this stage you should pay close attention to what the topic or question is asking you to do. The wording of essay topics usually suggests what the BOIs need to be.

⊙ Let your mind range freely, adding items of information, or points you wish to make, wherever they seem most relevant on your Mind Map. There is no limit to the number of branches and sub-branches that can radiate outwards from your BOIs. During this Mind Mapping stage you should use codes (colours, symbols, or both) to indicate cross-reference or association between different areas.

⊙ Next, edit and re-order your Mind Map into a cohesive whole.

⊙ Now sit down and write the first draft of your essay, using the Mind Map as a framework. A well-organized Mind Map should provide you with:

- All the main sub-divisions of your essay.
- The key points to be mentioned in each.
- The way those points relate to each other.

At this stage you should write as quickly as possible, skipping over any areas that cause you special difficulty, especially particular words or grammatical structures. In this way you will create a much greater flow, and you can always return to the 'problem areas' later, much as you would when studying a reference book.

⊙ If you come up against 'writer's block', (which with a Mind Map you probably won't – remember that jigsaw puzzle!), doing another Mind Map will help you overcome it. In many cases just drawing the central image will get your mind going again, playing and freewheeling round the topic of your essay. If you get blocked once more, simply add new lines branching off from the Key Words and Images you have so far generated, and your brain's natural Gestalt or 'completing' tendency will fill in the blank spaces with new words and images. At the same time you should remind yourself of your brain's infinite capacity for association and allow all your thoughts to flow, especially the ones you may have been dismissing as 'absurd'. Such blocks will disappear as soon as you realize that they are actually created not by your brain's inability but by an underlying fear of failure and a misunderstanding of the way your brain works.

⊙ Finally, review your Mind Map and put the finishing touches to your essay, adding cross-references, supporting your argument with more evidence or quotations, and modifying or expanding your conclusions where necessary.

Mind Mapping for examinations

Having taken Mind Map notes throughout your course of study, and having reviewed your Mind Maps at the recommended intervals, you should be more than ready for the examination. All you need to translate your excellent knowledge into excellent performance is the correct approach.

1   The first step is to read the examination paper fully, selecting the questions you choose to answer, noting in Mini-Mind Maps any thoughts that immediately spring to mind on reading the questions.

2   Next, you have to decide in what order you are going to answer the questions, and how much time you will devote to each.

3   Resisting the temptation to start answering the first question in detail straight away, do quick-fire Mind Map bursts on all the questions you intend to answer. By following this procedure, you enable your mind to explore, *throughout the examination*, the ramifications of all the questions regardless of

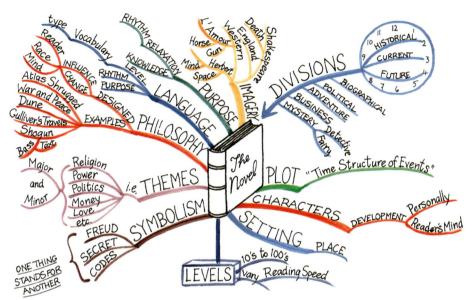

A Mind Map to help a literature student pass her exam (which she did!).

the particular question you are answering at any given time.

4 Now go back to your first question and do a Mind Map to act as the framework for your answer. The central image corresponds to your introductory comments, while each of the major branches provides a major subheading or section of the essay. For each extension from your major branches, you should be able to write a paragraph or two.

5 As you build up your answer you will find that you can begin to cross-refer throughout your knowledge structure, and can conclude by adding your own thoughts, associations and interpretations. Such an answer will demonstrate to the examiner a comprehensive knowledge, an ability to analyze, organize, integrate and cross-refer, and especially an ability to come up with your own creative and original ideas on the subject. In other words you will have achieved top marks!

Case study: Mind Map® in action

The Mind Map below is one of hundreds of Mind Maps by student James Lee. He prepared these Mind Maps to help him pass his senior and university entrance examinations. At the age of 15 James missed six months of schooling because of illness and was advised to go back a year in view of the fact that his 'O' level examinations loomed on the horizon. James persuaded his teachers to let him 'go for it' and started to Mind Map everything in sight! In just three months he did a year's work, and in ten examinations scored seven As and three Bs. This Mind Map is one that James did for History, outlining the main explanations given for the commencement of the Second World War.

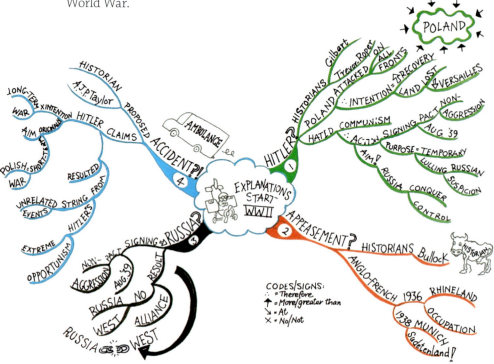

One of the Mind Maps by James Lee that helped him to pass his exams.

Limit your time, not your boundaries

College or university students, who take exams regularly, will find it very useful to write every essay to a strict time limit, as if it were an examination question. This approach is especially rewarding in highly competitive academic situations, where your brain needs constant training to excel under pressure-cooker examination conditions.

Swedish student Katarina Naiman used Mind Maps for essays on Sweden:

'The more I wrote and drew, the more things came to my mind – the more ideas I got, the more brave and original they were. I have realized that a Mind Map is never-ending. Only some other person I respect, a stomach aching of hunger, or real thirst could make me stop building my Mind Maps!'

Mind Mapping for group study

Study can also be a communal experience (as well as a solitary revision exercise) and Mind Maps are ideal for small groups seeking to increase their studying efficiency. Using well organized Mind Map notes, the content of a whole text book can be communicated to members of the group within one hour or less. I recommend a study day with, say, four members, in which four books can be read, Mind Mapped, understood and exchanged.

1 Start at 10 a.m. having had a half-hour exercise or stretching session.
2 Quickly browse through the text to be studied (15 minutes).
3 Break – rest, play games, relax (15 minutes).
4 Decide how much time you have available for study and

breaks, and divide it into chunks to cover appropriate sections of material (10 minutes).

5   Mind Map your existing knowledge of the subject, your goals and objectives, and the questions you want to answer (20 minutes).

6   Break (5–10 minutes).

7   Take a quick overview of your text book, looking at the contents, major headings and so on. Then put in the major branches on your Mind Map (15 minutes).

8   Preview your book, looking at the material in more detail, and continue building your Mind Map (15 minutes).

9   Lunch break (60 minutes).

10 This is the interview stage during which you can discuss and resolve your problem areas with others in your study group (30 minutes).

11 Break (5–10 minutes).

12 Review your book, dealing with any outstanding problems or questions and filling the final details on your Mind Map (30 minutes).

13 Break (5–10 minutes).

14 This is the exchange during which study group members present, from your own Mind Maps, a complete summary of what has been learned from your particular study text. Each presentation should last about 25 minutes with a 5–10 minute break after the first two. While one member presents, you should make your own Mind Maps and attempt to gain an understanding at least equal to that of the presenter. You should all be able to refine and improve each other's and your own Mind Maps to the highest possible level.

15 By 4 or 5 in the afternoon, you all have four new books of information in your head and the only thing you need to do with the actual text is to have a little browse through to add to your Mind Maps during the coming year.

⊙ You have achieved an enhanced knowledge of the subject through Mind Map communication, rather than via linear notes which diffuse the knowledge.

⊙ Moreover it has been a positive and enjoyable experience, completely different from the pain and punishment anxieties of study – so now go out and celebrate!

Benefits of group Mind Map® study

What percentage of the book do you think each one of your study group will have learned of, say, a book on geography which includes sections on weather systems, wildlife, geology, planetary maps and the like? Answer: 75 per cent.

An average student who reads a whole book, and takes ages to do that, absorbs between 60 and 80 per cent in an entire year and then forgets up to 80 per cent of it within a week. In other words, it is better to start 'cramming' at the *beginning* of the year. Why spend the whole of the year being terrified about the looming monstrous tsunami that is coming at you, and in 90 per cent of cases, is going to blow you away? Why wait until the last moment to stop it? Why don't you push it off the horizon right at the beginning?

The other advantage of group Mind Map study is that when your study group is sitting in the second week of lectures, you will be at the great advantage of already having all the main texts Mind Mapped. So when your lecturer starts to talk about a 'new topic for the week', you will already have anticipated it and have a clear Mind Map in your head before she even begins. Then, as she brings up interesting ideas, you can simply add them to your fabulous Mind Map. But it doesn't end there.

Whatever is said inside or outside the class, lecture hall, or tutorial in any way associated with that topic, your brain will have the ultimate network of the synapses to add and grow – '*snap! snap! snap!*' – like a fusion or fission reaction, a critical mass.

And that's just one subject. How many subjects does a student study? At this level, four, maybe five – so if there are 30 books you need to read in an academic year, and you are a gang of four, you can get through them in eight Saturdays, and by the end of the first two months of the academic year you've got it all bedded down.

Your future

Your mental armoury is now complete and you are equipped with a brain of extraordinary power. You have obliterated the standard obstacles to effective study. You are able to read faster than 99 per cent of the world's population. You have a newly supercharged memory. You have knowledge of the theory and application to study of the world's most powerful thinking, learning and memory tool, the Mind Map, and you know how to mobilize the most powerful studying technique, BOST, to your ultimate advantage.

I look forward to hearing about your exam success!

Answers

Page 95: Eye-cue vocabulary exercise – prefixes
1 prepare; 2 reviewing; 3 depress; 4 comprehension;
5 examinations

Page 97: Eye-cue vocabulary exercise – suffixes
1 practitioner; 2 hedonism; 3 minimal; 4 vociferous;
5 psychology

Page 99: Eye-cue vocabulary exercise – roots
1 querulous; 2 amiable; 3 equinox; 4 chronometer;
5 aerodynamics

Further reading

For those of you who are ready to take your knowledge beyond the arena of study, my Mind Set series contains in-depth guidance on how to make maximum use of your mind and your memory in all aspects of life. The following books are available from BBC Active:

Use Your Head
The Mind Map® Book
The Illustrated Mind Map® Book
The Speed Reading Book
Use Your Memory
Master Your Memory